KINGDOM AUTHORITY

Living your Life in Kingdom Power

PETRUS DE KLERK

2016
NEELY WORLDWIDE PUBLISHING
WASHINGTON D.C.

CONTENTS

TRANSLATIONS AND ABBREVIATIONS

The New King James translation is used for scripture references. With additional references, the following translations were used with abbreviation only.

Alf	The New Testament (Henry Alford)
AmP	The Amplified Bible
ASV	The American Standard Version.
Bas	The New Testament in Basic English
Beck	The New Testament in the Language of Today (William F. Beck)
Ber	The Berkeley Version of the New Testament (Gerrit Verkuyl)
Con	The Epistles of Paul (W.J. Conybeare)
DeW	A Rendering of the Book of Psalms (John DeWitt)
Gspd	The New Testament: An American Translation
Jerus	The Jerusalem Bible
KJV	King James Version
Knox	The New Testament in the Translation of Monsignor Ronald Knox
Lam	The Holy Bible From Ancient Eastern Manuscripts (George M. Lamsa)
Mes	The Message Bible
Mof	The New Testament: A Translation (James Moffatt)
Mon	The Centenary Translation: The New Testament in Modern English (Helen Barrett Montgomery)
Msg	Message Translation
NASB	The New American Standard Bible: New Testament
NEB	The New English Bible: New testament
NIV	New International Version
Nor	The New testament: A New Translation (Olaf M.Norlie)
Phi	The New Testament in Modern English (J.B.Phillips)
RIEU	The Four Gospels (E.V. Rieu)
Rhm	The Emphasized New Testament: A New Translation (J.B. Rotherham)
Sept	The Septuagint (Charles Thomson)
Tay	Living letters; Living Gospels; Living Prophecies (Kenneth N. Taylor)
TCNT	The Twentieth Century New Testament
Wey	The New Testament in Modern Speech (Richard Francis Weymouth)
Wms	The New Testament: A Translation in the Language of the People (Charles B. Williams)

AUTHORS PREFACE

I sincerely believe that we are entering a pivotal season as the church, wherein we will advance from our present spiritual position to a greater position of authority, abundance, success, and supernatural power here on earth. We need to completely surrender to the supreme King of the kingdom if we want to experience this reality.

The church needs to be transformed from a religious and self-focused institution into a dynamic force on the earth. *The kingdom of God* is being established by God to exhibit absolute sovereignty, accurate leadership, heavenly governance, and supernatural power.

The church is not just called to be busy with administration and social issues, but to influence governments, eliminate poverty and racism, and infiltrate nations by displaying the grace and glory of our Lord, Jesus Christ. The impossibility of perfection on the earth will soon become a genuine possibility, which will turn into an awesome reality.

The kingdom of God is at hand, and the revealing of the sons of God is imminent. The ambassadors of Christ will take their place with faith and authority. There will be no place for arrogance and pride, because the glory of the Lord will fill the earth. The ultimate victory that Jesus Christ obtained more than two thousand years ago will eventually be proclaimed in all the nations of the earth.

It is pivotal in God's heavenly agenda that we establish His kingdom here on earth. The King of kings, Jesus Christ, will reign supreme. And we will reign with Him.

The time for believing in man-made, self-focused, and unscriptural philosophies is coming to an end. Enough has been said about revival and awakenings. The church should enter into its divine calling. Our heavenly assignment is to possess the land, and to proclaim the victorious, never-ending, ever-increasing, indestructible kingdom of God.

- Petrus de Klerk

i

PRAISE FOR KINGDOM AUTHORITY

Pastor Johan Gericke
New Life Church
Ripon
North Yorkshire
United Kingdom
www.newliferipon.org.uk

'It is such an honor to share some thoughts about my dear friend and brother Petrus. We have spent amazing moments together in various meetings, conferences and golf courses. There was and still is such an excitement to spend time together with him and his family. There are many observations about the Kingdom and expressed ideas about the Kingdom but a small number perceive the intended meaning and live it out by example. Petrus is one of those people that live his believes by example. Petrus has a deep understanding of the prejudices and ignorance that have prevailed in the Body of Christ. The Kingdom culture concept that he so powerfully projects supersedes all other cultures and ushers in a new breed; those who have been kingdomized.' This is a timely scriptthat should be read prayerfully and allow the transformational power of this message to bring greater wisdom, knowledge and understanding in our lives.

Pastor Allan Rockhill
Kingsnet Ministries
Durban
South Africa
www.kingsnet.com

'I have known Petrus for over twenty years now and enjoyed watching the transformation in his own life, as he has endeavored to work out the lifestyle of a relationship with God that is real, down to earth and practical. Many profess the 'faith' but their actions don't justify the way they live. So many are caught up in religious mindsets and certain mechanical behavior that is expected of religious people. Just like the writing of this book, which challenges the religious way of life, Petrus portrays a faith that comes out of a real relationship with God that is simple and based on the Word of God. If God says it then it must be. He lives this way and demonstrates how easy it is to live for God and represent His Kingdom here on earth. This is a mark of those who know the difference.'

ACKNOWLEDGEMENTS

The faith that my family has displayed in me throughout the years is absolutely incredible. Without them I would never have been able to preach and teach so passionately. They never stopped believing in me as a man of God, and for this I am ever grateful.

Thank you Millanie, you are not just my most wonderful and beautiful wife, but also my kingdom partner and best friend. We are experiencing great things right now, but together we will continue to enjoy the greater things in the kingdom of God.

Thank you Wiehann and Chérie, you are not just the best children that God could give Mom and me, but I believe you will advance everything written in this book to a higher level of completion and perfection in the kingdom of God. You are kingdom warriors, and ambassadors of Jesus, the Christ of God. You are called to inherit every spiritual benefit that I have received, and run with the kingdom vision of generational increase and blessings.

Thank you Albert, Arianne, and Kirsten; for you have spent many hours on the editing of all the pages in the 'Kingdom Authority'. I appreciate you sincerely.

Most of all, I thank you, Father God, for beginning a good work in me. I am so thankful that this work is not completed yet, and that you are still giving me more opportunities to advance your kingdom here on earth. I know you are not finished with Petrus de Klerk, and that the best for me is yet to come.

1

A MULTICULTURAL KINGDOM

Growing up on a cattle and corn farm in South Africa was fantastic. We had a wonderful farmhouse, and my grandparents lived in their own separate farmhouse, which was about a hundred meters from our own. I knew what freedom was, always running freely and widely with my dog, and riding my bicycle for many miles.

As an eleven-year-old boy, I had my own chickens, and I literally spent hours looking after them. My Father was a busy farmer and my Mother was a teacher at the local country school. I had the luxury of driving to school with her in one of our vehicles. Talking about vehicles, I remember us always having two cars, a utility vehicle, a truck, a few tractors, as well as a number of farming implements. We even had our own tennis court as well as a concrete farm dam for our own leisure. We had orchards, creeks, warehouses, trees, hills, and many open fields.

On our way to school on weekdays, we often passed groups of black kids running bare feet to their own little school. All the farmers had heaps of black people working on their farms and the kids were appearing from everywhere as we were driving. I recall the determination on their faces. They were eager to get to school, carrying some old books in plastic bags.

I remember how I played soccer on our farm with my black friends. We were great mates and we had no apparent racial issues. We just played together on the farm. We never went to school, church, or movies together. We never even talked about the possibility of having a meal together. We never had a swim together, drove together in a truck or even went to church together. Everything was separate; black and white. We were conditioned to live and think this way. We grew up in a season of total discrimination by a minority group over a majority group, within one nation. I never found this strange, and I never asked any questions about this. I think we were just conditioned to accept things the way they were. The underlining message was that we were different.

I never felt sorry for these kids. This is how life was. This is all I knew. I was happy, and they too seemed to be content. I never thought that this could be unjust, cruel, corrupt or even unlawful in any society. My parents and grandparents were committed Christians and we regularly went to church and Sunday school. We prayed before every meal. I was just a child having a genuinely good life, growing up in a very decent home. But without having real understanding about the issues of life, a new generation of racists was formed. As the saying goes: "Like father, like son."

I don't remember any 'hate' conversations at home as such and, nothing felt wrong or innately evil. I guess we were all like frogs in a pot of warm water- not realizing that we are slowly but surely being boiled. I would become a person with racial prejudice; a person who would think like everybody else; a person who would not be flexible and willing to change his ways. I would become a typical white farmer's son who didn't like black people.

Our lifestyles were fixed. We lived under a government that was set in its ways of separation and discrimination. The white minority government acknowledged God in many ways but still conditioned society into the false reality of separation. Such intimidation was devious and crafty, and was supported through a totally partial media association. Even the education department, sport groups, and church leaders, approved of this cruel regime. There was no clear public outcry towards this separation policy. I cannot recall the voice of a black politician, preacher, or even an artist from my childhood. These voices were silent in white communities, and white society.

We were taught that white and black people just don't mix together, and we were conditioned that this is the way God intended things to be; a Christian philosophy to trust and to support. The government made this biased, immoral, discriminatory, and shameful system the law of the day.

The schools implemented this system as a regulation. The churches proclaimed this system as suitable. Our own parents approved of this unjust system. We never really gave this cruel, prejudice system a name, until somebody, somewhere, called it 'Apartheid'.

After playing a game of soccer, my friends would be off to their humble villages, miles from our magnificent farmhouse. They accepted the fact that I was the superior authority because of my skin color. They called me 'boss', like they would do with every other white person. They couldn't break any of my rules. I mean, my Grandfather gave their parents a hiding with a whip if they didn't obey his orders promptly. How could they even try to question my rules in a game? How could they ever oppose me? All they said was: "Good morning boss, thank you boss, yes boss!"

————————————

Separatism was rife. Black people couldn't enter white people's churches, cafes, shops, and even beaches. I remember how black families were escorted from the beautiful beaches of Kwa-Zulu Natal by the Police Force when they had dared to come for a swim. They had to be on the look out for 'Whites

Only' signs on buses, trains, and toilet facilities. The cities had a 'clock' rule that forced all black people to exit the city at a certain time at night. They had to rush after work to get to their townships. These townships were far away from the 'white' cities and it could take these tired workers hours to get to their homes.

We were living in a society of total ignorance and exclusion, wherein many cultural groups were openly belittled. This degrading was inhuman and can be described as utter disrespect for a fellow human being. I truly believe that there must have been some exceptions to the racial attitude of most people. As I have described however, I never observed any behavior less than one of harshness towards black people. It was the norm in our society. *South Africa was multicultural, but completely segregated in its diversity.*

At the funeral of a white person, the black people were only allowed to stand on the other side of a fence to show their respect. I remember being moved to tears at the end of a particular funeral by the amazing singing of a group of farm workers. They always showed respect to white folk and did not deserve to be treated in the manner which they were.

Because of a different skin color, black people could not sign up for military training in South Africa, and were not allowed to become members of sport clubs, and consequently could never dream of playing for their national team. Yes, we lived a nightmare. More than eighty percent of the people in my country were categorized as black, and none of them could even cast a vote in an election.

I thank the Lord today for the transformations that occurred in my country of birth during the last few decades. History shows that 'Apartheid' has fallen, and that democracy has emerged. Although it will take many more decades for all the pain to be healed, we thank God for the 'Nelson Mandelas' and the 'F.W. de Klerks' of this world. I would ask every person who reads this book to persist in praying for this amazing country.

Even though I came to know Christ as my Lord and Savior in 1983, my mindset was still set on the 'solid rock' of 'Apartheid'. At that time my Christian lifestyle and connections were not yet multicultural at all. Somehow I still found a way to approve of this wrong system of separation. Sadly, nobody mentored me through this process. Most friends I had at this stage of my life were just as ignorant about this issue as I was. We just decided to go with the flow and basically 'hate' black people. We didn't talk about it. Nobody within my circle made an effort to put an end to it either.

Being very passionate to testify about the great work Christ has started in me, people regularly responded by challenging me about my 'segregation philosophy'. Things were made even worse by myself, as I had a strong conviction that the separation of people was biblically correct. This is how I was operating in the days of my youth. I was on fire for God, but prejudice and racism were still prominent in my world. *Our beloved Republic of South Africa needed a miracle from God. I needed a miracle from God!*

Millanie Pretorius and I got married in September 1989. During the early stages of our marriage, our lives basically consisted of work, church, and caring for our two dogs. We were excited about life as we just bought our first house with a swimming pool! We both had good jobs, we were involved in the worship team at church, and we were the youth leaders of a group of some seventy teenagers. I also studied part time to become a pastor, and life was busy and exciting. The Lord also confirmed to us in this time that He had a special assignment for the two of us.

One night I had a dream. It wasn't a long dream, but it was real. In my dream I experienced the life of a black man in the Apartheid era. God was giving me another perspective on life. He was showing me the other side of the coin. I was the same person in the dream but I existed in another culture and in another skin. I lived the life of a black man- a life submitted to intimidation and unfair treatment.

5

I experienced the discrimination and the harassment. I felt the torture of racial resentment and the fear of bashing. It was like the highlights of a horror movie, the difference being that this was personal and tangible. It was like a snapshot of my entire life- a life that I wasn't living, but could have lived. Every moment in this dream was devastating, including the prejudice and all the abuse a black human being might have to endure. I felt the pain and the bitterness. Anguish and fear took hold of me. I experienced the hopelessness of racial abuse, and the reality of a lifestyle that represents poverty and inferiority.

I awakened in sweat. I was shocked and distressed as if the dream was a real life event. My life would never be the same again. I never had an experience quite similar to this one. God often speaks to me in other ways, but not really in dreams, but this dream was about to change my life. God gave me a new heart.

The immediate result of my life-changing dream was that I have received an indescribable love for all people from all cultures and backgrounds.

This moment was pivotal for my future undertakings. All decisions, plans, ambitions, and ministry enterprises that I would ever pursue, would now have the heartbeat of all- inclusiveness. Prejudice, racial partiality, and cultural bias were gone. It vanished in a flash. *It took God one night, one moment, one dream, to reconstruct my distorted opinions.*

I don't view this as a nightmare or a warning from God. It was more a spiritual transformation; an operation; a heart transplant. It is truly amazing how God works in mysterious ways. Imagine how dark my life could have turned out to be if I never had experienced this moment.

Bileam's donkey saved the prophet's life when he saw the angel with the sword. *(Numbers 22:21-39)* My 'donkey' was a dream that stopped me from continuing along the path of racism and prejudice. I am totally convinced that God is color-blind. He loves and accepts all people. His kingdom includes all nations, cultures, and tribes. His kingdom is multicultural.

My own children had the privilege of growing up in a new way of thinking and living; they can't even believe my childhood stories. The generational curse of separation and prejudice was totally broken. Everything has changed for my family, and I just knew that our country was on the brink of a similar miracle.

Many people had different encounters with God during these times. We could sense that God was preparing the church in South Africa for a huge shift towards the inclusion of all people. The previously strong fortresses of the old regime started to fall as God was working behind the scenes to bring amazing change to an amazing land.

Imagine people getting jobs, ministry opportunities, promotions, college scholarships, and selection to sports teams, on the condition of a specific skin color. This prejudice will never be tolerated in the kingdom of God. This would be totally against the heartbeat of heaven. I am totally convinced that there are no exceptions to this rule in the kingdom of God. Governments, educational institutions, sports organizations and even businesses may still get away with this animosity, but we cannot overlook any form of bias in the kingdom of God. It is wrong, it is a sin, and we have to take responsibility for who we are and what we stand for. Prejudice is ignorance. We live in a society filled with information and new technology. There are just no excuses for ignorance anymore, especially for the church of Jesus Christ on the earth. We represent what is correct, accurate, and perfect. We represent God and heaven.

———————————-

Revelations 7:9,10 After these things I looked, and behold, a great multitude which no one could number, of all nations,* tribes, peoples, and tongues, standing before the throne and before the Lamb, clothed with white robes, with palm branches *in their hands, and crying out with a loud voice, saying, 'Salvation belongs to our God who sits on the throne, and to the Lamb!'*

* From every nation, tribe, people, and language. (Gspd)

God made man (humans) in His image. God is love. He loves all people equally. His unique plan was for all men to live in unity and peace. The devastating effect of sin led to people starting to hate each other because of differences in background, philosophies, traditions, and skin color. Many wars have started because people just couldn't agree about certain (little) things.

Bias is based on facts. Being biased towards any other person only displays that a person is wrongly informed, and that his mindset needs transformation. We have to make a determined effort to display heavenly and cultural harmony. We are here to influence the distorted worldly ideologies, and penetrate the darkness of cultural and racial predjudice.

During the next phase of my life, I had the privilege of making many friends from different cultural backgrounds. Doors were opened for me to minister in many townships in South Africa. These townships were the cities of the black people. I was invited to travel to the heartland of Zambia where I have gained apostolic oversight over many churches. I made many friends with pastors and their struggling churches. These wonderful people were living in poverty at the time, yet they were so gracious to us, always giving us the best accommodation and food in the most extreme of situations.

It all felt like a reconnection with my roots. Building new friendships with all these families reminded me of my early days when I was playing soccer on the farm with my black friends. The change of heart that took place in my life resulted into a new chapter of multi-cultural experiences.

Waking after the dream and actually stepping into the perfect heartbeat of multi-faceted relationships, brought total fulfillment for my family and me. *I could talk with any person, have a meal with them, laugh with them, and hug them. Cultural differences disappear in the kingdom of God.*

It took us ten years to establish a multicultural church in our community in Durban. It was shocking to see how people opposed the idea of complete multicultural thinking. People would be happy if you talk about doing things together as different cultural groups. But people would be shaken to the core if you asked them if a pastor with black skin could stay at their house. The excuses these folk offered were numerous. We had to leave certain organizations as we stepped into the purposes and plans of God for our own lives.

When we decided to immigrate to Australia, we fare-welled a church that was multicultural to the core. From a church which only consisted of white people that only wanted to sing in Afrikaans in 1997, we were able to leave a church in 2007 that was totally transformed. There were Indians, Zambians, Congolese, Zulus, Afrikaans and English speaking white folk- a representation of the wonderful variety of God's people.

We should never look at the skin color of people; we have to simply and purely embrace their hearts. The black pastors who invited me to preach, looked after me as if I was a king. They carried my Bible and gave me water and soft drinks while I was preaching. They couldn't wait for me to pray for them and for their people. This is what friendship, respect, and love really is.

I gained more black friends than I lost white ones. Yes, I was judged, mocked and criticized. But the most that my old life could offer could never compare with the love, grace, and satisfaction of embracing a multi-cultural lifestyle. As the church we can never again allow forced authority, white supremacy, or blatant racism in any shape or form. It opposes the heartbeat of our Creator.

KINGDOM AUTHORITY

God's heart is multicultural and He loves all nations equally. We are so blessed to be the New Testament Israel of God in Christ. We do not have to travel to Jerusalem to gain the favor of our God. In God's eyes we are golden vessels who carries His glory. We are not really Chinese, Australian, Norwegian, Indian, or Italian people.

We are the people of God. Being Mexican, Scottish, Sudanese or even Jewish in this life can only mean a real blessing if you are born again into the kingdom of God. God is building Himself a kingdom from every nation, tongue, and tribe. God is multicultural and He is the President of His multicultural, ever-increasing kingdom.

2

IN CHRIST

I gave my life to the Lord Jesus Christ in 1983 as a nineteen-year-old student. A close friend of mine was in a horrifying vehicle accident during a wild party. I still remember being invited to drive with another student to buy more alcohol. However, I wasn't so keen to go, as I had my eyes on a particular young lady at the party. It was through the grace of God that I never got into that car. Yet a friend of mine, decided to go. Later that evening we heard the news that these two young men had driven into a tree at 140 kph. They were both under the influence of alcohol and narrowly escaped death.

The shock had a massive impact on many people's lives, mine included. At this stage of my life I was spiritually blindfolded and consequently, looking for answers in all the wrong places. Reflecting on that horrific night I couldn't help thinking that I was the person who should have been sitting in the passenger seat. I felt that God had spared me and was clearly speaking to me through this incident. Around this time a friend shared the gospel with me.

KINGDOM AUTHORITY

Although I grew up in a Christian home and went to church regularly, I never made a personal commitment to Christ. But on that particular day I accepted Jesus Christ as my Savior. It was a very real and emotional experience for me. My life has never been the same; I could never have imagined how a modest decision could change the course of my life in such a profound manner.

Soon after my conversion I was baptized in water. I remember that day as if it were yesterday. A friend from my student days, Wessel van Rheede van Oudtshoorn, posted a photo of my baptism in Potchefstroom on a social media network recently, along with the words: 'This was a historical moment'. And it was!

Wessel's post helped me remember this pivotal moment in my life when I celebrated the relocation of my life from the kingdom of darkness into the kingdom of light and love. Today I can testify to the unique privilege of being established in Christ. My love and passion for Him have increased over the years. Such an experience defies all human logic.

2 Corinthians 5:17 Therefore, if anyone is in Christ, he is a new creation; old things have passed away; *Behold, all things have become new.

* His old life has passed away, a new life has begun! (TCNT)

* The past is finished and gone, everything has become fresh and new. (Phi)

As mentioned, I grew up in a Christian home, and I remain grateful to my parents for raising me in a God-honoring environment, yet my new experience was a huge challenge for them too because I was the first person in my family to be baptized in water as a believer. I was also the first one to be baptized in the Holy Spirit with the evidence of speaking in tongues. It was challenging for my family to understand the

12

reality of my life-transforming encounter with God.

These were pioneering moments for me. Little did I know I would one day be a local pastor, plant a church, baptize hundreds of people, tutor in a Bible School and even teach in a Christian School in another country. I mention these things only to bring glory to God for bringing salvation, freedom and forgiveness into my world, and doing more with me than I could have ever asked or even imagined. The old life of sin and shame is indeed gone. Meeting Jesus Christ was the best thing that could ever have happened to me. And by the grace of God I can declare today with Joshua in *Joshua 24:15b: 'But as for me and my household, we will serve the Lord'. (NIV)*

Everything changes if we are in Christ:

- We are called out of the kingdom of darkness into the marvelous kingdom of light.
- We are new people in a new world. This new world is the reality of the incredible kingdom of God.
- We were sinners but now we are forgiven. We were lost but now we are found. All our sins are thrown into the depths of the sea.
- We were far away from God but now we are close to His mercy and love. We abide in His presence.
- We are born again by the grace of God. There is no way we can go back to where we came from. Everything is new.
- We are a heavenly species—a new creation. We are aliens to the worldly system of sin and darkness. We are foreigners in this world because we have received the citizenship of heaven.
- We bring a new world-order into this realm. God is transforming us into the image of His Son Jesus Christ so that we can transform this world into His image as well.

God made us new creations, so that we can make creation new. A newborn baby changes a household completely. We have entered the kingdom living through Christ, by the grace of God. We are now compelled to tell the world of His grace and love for mankind.

————————

Rom 8:1 There is therefore now no condemnation* to those who are in Christ Jesus.

* The conclusion of the matter is this: there is now no condemnation for those who are united with (in) Christ Jesus. (NEB)

The late Nelson Mandela made the following statement when he was released from prison after serving a twenty-seven year sentence: 'No one is born hating another person because of the color of his skin, or his background, or his religion. People must learn to hate, and if they can learn to hate, they can be taught to love, for love comes more naturally to the human heart than its opposite.'

As Christians we know this is true because God has created us in His image, and He is love. If we are born with the capacity to love, and as Mandela says; 'must be taught to hate', then these limitations exist mainly in our thought life. *In Christ, all spiritual prison bars are broken. In Him, mindsets of destruction, failure and poverty are demolished.*

Nelson Mandela chose love over hate, and forgiveness over revenge. After so many years behind prison bars, he displayed the reality of freedom through love. In Christ all prison doors are supernaturally opened. We can run free. We are free indeed; body, soul, and spirit. All we need to do is to accept the freedom. It is a choice.

Paul and Silas experienced the condemnation of the severe legalistic and political systems of their time. They were unjustly sentenced to prison. *(Acts 16)* In the midst of their trial and tribulation in a prison cell —with feet fastened in stocks —they decided to sing praises to God. While the other prisoners were listening to them, a violent earthquake shook the foundations of the prison and the doors were opened and all of the prisoners' chains were loosed. This supernatural miracle brought freedom to Paul and Silas, as well as salvation to the prison guard and his household.

Violent heavenly earthquakes are about to shake the foundations of sin, shame, darkness and demons. The kingdom of God is a dimension that brings supernatural results. Religious foundations will be shaken and the chains of legalism will be broken. Condemnation will be superseded by grace. Prison doors will open and people will be able to walk free again.

Peter miraculously escaped from prison when the angel of the Lord appeared on the scene. *(Acts 12)* Peter was sleeping between two soldiers, bound with two chains, and surrounded by guards. His chains fell off and he followed the angel to the gate. The prison gate opened supernaturally. Nothing could hold Peter in prison.

Chains of bitterness, anger, judgement, and hatred will not be able to bind us any longer when we choose to live in the perfection of God's kingdom. The angels of God are busy removing solid chains from our spiritual lives. Gates of iron that kept us confined in dark prisons of depression, poverty, doubt and inferiority are being opened in the heavenly realm at this very moment. *The strong gates of legalism and religious tradition that prevent people to enter into this perfect kingdom will soon break open. If Christ has set us free, we are free indeed.*

Rom 8:37 Yet in all these things we are more than conquerors* through Him who loved us.

* In all these things we win an overwhelming victory through Him who has proved his love for us. (Phi)

Life is not supposed to be a competition, but a process of completion. We are more than conquerors through Jesus Christ, but we need to sit the tests of life to advance to the next level. There is no way Jesus Christ will just leave us in our current state of existence. He wants us to live life to the full and complete the journey victoriously; He is working with us to bring us to this state of completion. He will present us to the Father, blameless and complete.

The unity of God's people on the earth is a huge threat to the kingdom of darkness. There are no agreement amongst devils and demons. Our unity with Christ, and with one another announces us as the overwhelming champions of the world. No other kingdom owns this perfect unity. We don't compete, but we complete one another with all our different gifts and talents. We are champions and we remain victorious. It doesn't matter what others think or say. God's word declares that we are the undisputed champions of the world.

————————————-

2 Corinthians 5:21 For He made Him who knew no sin to be sin for us, that we might become the righteousness of God* in Him.

* So that through union with Him, we might come into right standing with God. (Wms)
* So that in Christ we might be made good with the goodness of God. (Phi)

The world is a tough place to live in. People are under constant pressure in the workplace, at home and in all areas of life. Corporate demands, social pressure, and media influences are becoming more severe every day. People are compelled to buy certain brands of clothes, specific models of vehicles, and expensive properties in particular locations. As kingdom people we do not have to bow to these pressures. We are blessed with the knowledge that we are in right standing with God. We are 'right' before Him. He views us as good and wonderful.

His goodness will lead us through the tough times. We are designed to repel pressure, overcome difficult situations and live victoriously in this tough world. It is important to realize that we have already received this position of righteousness and goodness with God. It is not a futuristic hope at all, but a current reality. There is nothing we can do to fail this position of union with God in Christ because it has been sealed by Christ's death and resurrection.

Romans 8:38,39 For I am persuaded that neither death nor life, nor angels nor principalities, nor powers, nor things present nor things to come, nor height nor depth, nor any other created thing shall be able to separate us from the love of God which is in Christ Jesus our Lord.

Jesus is the head of the church and we are His body. *(Ephesians 1:22,23)* In the natural world, separation between a head and body leads to immediate death. In the kingdom of God, the love of God protects us from any form of separation. Our God represents life!

Death, and anything that relates to it, cannot exist in the kingdom of God because Jesus Christ conquered death at Calvary. His kingdom reveals love, light, peace, and eternal connection with God. No power, even if it is launched from the pit of hell itself, can separate us from the river of love that flows from the throne of God.

The god of this world; the prince of darkness, will do his utmost to attach his worldly standards to us. The devil is the father of all lies; he separates, divides, discourages, steals and destroys. As a former angel who has experienced supreme authority in heaven, the devil now operates from a position of powerless frustration and confusion. His plans and schemes are no longer effective.

Under the new covenant that has been written for us in the blood of Jesus, we are no longer slaves to this old master, and his efforts to separate us from the love of God have been made null by the incredible sacrifice and finished work of Jesus. The devil is defeated and he now functions from a position of subtle craftiness. He can only influence us if we allow his cunning strategies to mislead or intimidate us. In Christ we find total security because nothing can separate us from the love of God, which is in Christ Jesus, our Lord.

Ephesians 2:4-6 But God made us alive together with Christ, and raised us up together, and made us sit together in the heavenly places* in Christ Jesus.

* And enthroned us with Him in the heavenly realm as being in Christ Jesus. (Wey)
* Made us sit down with Him in heaven. (Gspd)

Ephesians 2:13 But now in Christ Jesus you who once were far off have been brought near by the blood of Christ.

We are close to God. We are with Him and He is with us. We have to understand that God made a way and He prepared a place of intimacy for us (His people). As kingdom people we have to recognize our formidable position. We are in this position because of the grace of God and the blood of Jesus Christ. God sits on His heavenly throne, with Jesus Christ positioned at the right hand of the Father. In Christ we are now seated with Him in this glorious dimension. This is our seat of authority.

Jesus mentioned that He would declare our names in heaven, if we would be willing to declare His name on earth. We have the privilege of being known in heaven. Our position is not one of arrogance because we are in this position purely by His grace. However, we have the opportunity to use our heavenly power to influence earth.

We have received an inheritance through Christ Jesus that produces heavenly benefits for us in the kingdom of God here on earth. We make our decisions about work, finances, church, and relationships from this heavenly position. We cannot afford to operate from a merely human position as the church. We have to live from a position that seeks to see earth reflect the way things are above, in heaven. This position demonstrates grace, and not selfish ambition. This position declares God's authority and finality; it does not declare confusion and fear.

Closeness to God does not represent arrogance, but relational intimacy. It is a tangible closeness, solid and real. We cannot see it, but we believe it, we feel it, we know it. We can experience intimacy with God every day. *The blood of Jesus Christ took us from a place outside of an earthly tabernacle we were unworthy to enter, to a place very near to God, so near that He has chosen to dwell in us by His Holy Spirit. Heaven is closer than we think.*

Colossians 2:10 And you are complete* in Him, who is the head of all principality and power.

* Filled full. (Alf)
* So you have everything when you have Christ, and you are filled with God through your union with Christ. (Tay)
* And in Him you have your Fullness. (Con)

To have Jesus Christ in our inner world is the ultimate reality. There is absolutely no amount of money that can compare with the wealth of His majesty. There is no level of fame that can give us satisfaction like a relationship with Christ. There is no power or principality that can compare with the supernatural impartation of the amazing grace we have received by being in Jesus Christ.

He brings perfection to His kingdom, because He is the perfect King. We are truly complete in Christ. We are filled with God himself.

God does not operate with a demerit system. He generously gives us gifts and He will never take them away. God keeps on giving us everything even when we disobey Him, when we have little faith, or when we are following our own plans and desires. He gives unmerited favor (grace upon grace). We deserved nothing, but we have received everything in Christ.

2 Timothy 1:8,9 God, who has saved us and called us* with a holy calling, not according to our works, but according to His own purpose and grace which was given to us in Christ Jesus before time began.

* And called us with a call for dedication. (Ber)
* And from him we received our solemn Call. (TCNT)

We are all called with an amazing purpose for our lives. We are full-time ministers of the gospel of the kingdom. Pastors, evangelists and missionaries were traditionally seen as 'full-time workers' in the kingdom of God. This is a misconception, because God calls students, cleaners, teachers, pilots, chefs, accountants, soldiers, nurses, attorneys, single-mothers, and people of all professions, to a full-time commitment in ministry.

As God's people, we are first and foremost called to minister to Him. Our first priority in life is to honor this calling. When we live life to the full (using our talents and abilities), we are honoring the holy calling for which God has equipped us. We can't all be preachers, but it really doesn't matter. The Most Holy God calls us for a most holy purpose.

We are not just saved so that we can go to heaven. We are called out of the kingdom of darkness into God's amazing kingdom to shine forth His marvelous light. We are called to transform worldly systems and kingdoms. This is why Jesus taught His disciples to pray: 'Let your kingdom come... on earth as it is in heaven'. We are called to shape the future of our children, to bring God's blessings into this realm for the benefit of future generations. In Christ, we are called to influence the world with the power of God.

3

KINGDOM LIFESTYLE

My dear mother always said I would one day be either a rugby commentator or an auctioneer. She obviously recognized my ability to talk a lot. Well, I grew up to become a teacher and a preacher, and I am talking ever since!

I have never anticipated how things would unfold, in fact, how they are still unfolding. In 2006, I was given a prophetic word from the Lord about migrating to Australia with my family. God confirmed it clearly and we realized that this was not a suggestion or a man-made idea, but that He actually wanted us to relocate from South Africa to Australia.

Both my family and I said yes to the Lord. We, however, did not understand the change, stress, planning, faith, pain and joy that this decision to obey God, would involve. Well, we have now been living in Australia for about eight years and here I am, teaching at an International Christian School in Adelaide. Here I am, exploring new places and opportunities in this wonderful country. My children are pursuing their dreams and both have already travelled the world. And here I am, writing books!

KINGDOM AUTHORITY

Revelation 11:15 The kingdoms of this world* have become the kingdoms of our Lord and of His Christ, and He shall reign forever and ever.

*The sovereignty of the world now belongs to our Lord and His Christ. (Wey)
* The rule of the world. (Mof)
* The dominion of the world. (Knox)
* Has now come into the possession and become the kingdom of our Lord. (Amp)

Living in the kingdom could be defined as walking an exciting pathway with God into the future. It includes taking risks and making heaps of mistakes. It includes many monumental moments of victory and success. It is never boring as your life unfolds chapter by chapter, and as you walk with the King of the kingdom.

Jeremiah 1:5 Before I formed you in the womb I knew you; Before you were born I sanctified you; I ordained you* a prophet to the nations.

* I chose you, and I set you apart. (Mof)
* I knew and approved of you [as my chosen instrument]. (Amp)
* And appointed you as My spokesman to the world. (Tay)

Jeremiah's response to this amazing call from God was one of disbelief. He recognized that he was too young for this challenge and that he struggled to accomplish public speaking. *(Jeremiah 1:6)* The wonderful thing is that Jeremiah went on to conquer his feelings of inadequacy by eventually becoming a prophet of God to the nations.

We should never underestimate what God can do with us, or where he can take us. We are appointed and anointed by God for a specific assignment, but we need to respond to His calling with absolute obedience. Then, as we take our little steps of faith, He guides us into the future. As we trust Him and take action, amazing provision and clarity unfold.

To see the door to an amazing adventure open, we need to take the first step of obedience to God's prophetic, wise, and timely instructions. If we don't, we might never experience the reality of His wonderful plans for our life. They will remain a mystery, a distant possibility, or merely a dream. The only way to find out if the kingdom lifestyle is real is to step out of your current position and, by faith, enter the domain of God's promises for your life.

God is not a man that He would lie. He does not change like shifting shadows. He is constant and consistently good and therefore His promises are good and secure. Following His instructions is not only safe and exiting, but can also be rather challenging. If we say no, and make excuses, we will struggle to enter the kingdom lifestyle. Saying 'Yes, Lord', is essential to move into our rightful position and enjoy kingdom living.

God has planned an amazing future for each one of us. He sets us up for success, not failure. There is hope and peace for us, both for today and tomorrow, whether we have gotten off to a good start or not. Jeremiah had a very humble beginning in ministry. In fact, he wasn't keen on starting his journey with God at all. But God chose him for greatness. The only thing that can hinder us from progressing on our life's journey is our own headspace. If we choose to believe God's promises we can experience the fulfillment of our destiny in this life. Kingdom living is about more than just getting to the destination; we can actually enjoy the journey. The destination is merely the end result of a particular season in our lives.

When we arrive at certain destinations in God, we will receive instructions to pursue new assignments. This is all part of our future in God. This God-cycle will continue as long as we are functioning in the kingdom of God. This cycle of pursuing our destiny and progressing in the kingdom will only end on the day we finish our earthly assignments; and even then, God may just surprise us with brand new assignments on a brand new earth and in a brand new heaven.

————————————

Many characters in the Bible were just like we are today; ordinary people living ordinary lives. Most of them had some sort of imperfection that could have made them see themselves as God's second or third choice. Some couldn't talk properly, others didn't have any leadership qualities, and there were those who were disobedient and arrogant; and some were even tainted by the most heinous of crimes. The good news is that God looks at our hearts. If we put our hand up to do something for Him, He will take it and lead us to the great future He has in store for us.

Joseph was a spoiled dreamer who was the apple of his father's eye. He annoyed his ten older brothers so much that they threw him in a pit and then sold him into slavery just to get rid of him. His life fell apart as he was falsely accused of attempted rape and ended up in prison. He never stopped dreaming and became the prince of Egypt, a mighty ruler in the land; second only to Pharaoh.

Moses was a murderer in exile who became the man who led God's people out of slavery. He brought hope and life to a people who were at the point of desperation and hopelessness. The people blamed him, criticized him and wanted him out of leadership, but he never gave up or returned to his old life. Moses was a stutterer but later in his life influenced thousands by speaking the truth with accuracy and fluency, despite his speech impediment. It was this man who said he could barely speak, who delivered the law of God to the people. When he started out, he needed his brother Aaron to be his voice in Egypt, but he matured into a spokesperson confident to deliver the words of the living God with authority and power.

David was a murderer and adulterer, but he is called a man after God's own heart and is known as the most influential worship songwriter of all time. He influenced his generation, and his intimate worship songs are still inspiring people today. He stepped up into the purposes of God despite committing murder and adultery. David is the ultimate example of someone who was once dominated by sin, but later totally forgiven and transformed by the grace of God.

Esther was an orphan in exile in a foreign land with no one in her life except for a God-fearing uncle. Against all odds, Esther rose to the occasion and was appointed as the queen of the nation. Through her boldness and strength, the nation of Israel was saved from total destruction.

The Seductive Samaritan woman (with five previous husbands) who was living with another man, became the evangelist who introduced her village to Jesus. On a particular day she was just going through the routine of gathering water for her camels, not knowing her life would change forever. A conversation with Jesus brought conviction, grace and salvation into her world. She repented of her previous lifestyle and went back to her city to testify about the man who gave her living water. Many were saved because of her encounter with Jesus.

Four desperate and despised lepers, who were outcasts in their society, decided to enter the enemy's camp to see if they could find something to eat—they had nothing to lose but their worthless lives. Everybody else had fled the area, thinking that the enemy was still standing strong. God worked behind the scenes as these lepers put their plan into action, thinking: 'Let's add one last crazy thing to our bucket list'. Astonishingly, they stepped into the war zone expecting to die, only to find that the enemy has been defeated. The outcast lepers became instant folk heroes when they announced God's amazing victory to the people.

In *Matthew 16:23* Jesus called *Peter* 'Satan' because he was trying to prevent the purposes of God in the earth. He was the quick-tempered disciple prone to dramatic reactions. He even tried to prevent the soldiers from arresting Jesus by attacking one of them with a sword. Luckily Peter wasn't the best sword fighter and just sliced an ear off one of them. Jesus came to the rescue of the soldier, but was very upset with Peter.

Peter was a coward, afraid to acknowledge Jesus publicly. Nevertheless, within a year after his spinelessness, he preached to a huge crowd and saw three thousand people coming to Christ. He became a courageous man of God who preached boldly and healed the sick in the name of Jesus Christ. Though Peter was a work in progress, he found a way to move past his nature and became the rock that Jesus built His church on. In all of his 'ups and downs', Peter once put His faith into action and walked on the water towards Jesus. Not many people have done that. It is time for us to look unto Jesus and walk on water. We may fail, but we should give it a go!

——————————————-

Revelation 5:10 And have made us kings and priests to our God; and we shall reign* on the earth.

* And didst make them a Kingdom of Priests in the service of our God, and they are reigning upon the earth. (TCNT)
* And You have made them a kingdom [royal race] and priests to our God, and they shall reign [as kings] over the earth! (Amp)

We are designed to worship and to reign. Adam and Eve were given the authority to have dominion over everything upon the earth. They lost that authority through their poor choices, but this authority has now been restored to us through the perfect Adam, Jesus Christ our Lord, who redeemed it on our behalf. He has made us kings. We are kings of the King.

Jesus Christ is our Chief, our Leader, our King and the High Priest of our lives. He decided to delegate His sovereign power and supernatural dominion to His people. Jesus Christ has imparted His authority to us and we can willingly accept, or arrogantly ignore this token of trust. We are His designated authority in the earth; He has ordained and commissioned us. God created each of us as unique individuals. We are hand picked by Him to complete a specific assignment. We are ordained to live a victorious life on planet earth.

We are not designed to be battlers—people who just try to make ends meet, hoping to survive. We live in frustration if all we do is just going through the motions, longing for an imaginary ship to sail into our lives with all the answers to all our problems on board. We are designed to be imitators of the Creator—made in His image to be strong, influential, creative, purposeful, powerful, innovative and energetic.

Misdirected guilt about sin that has already been atoned for, and unjustified feelings of shame, will prevent us from believing that we can think and act like our Father. Even religious ideas, adherence to man-made standards (that do not take into account the amazing grace of God to those who are in Christ), and false humility, can influence us to pursue a poverty, survival- or escape-mentality.^

^ We may think that a *poverty mentality* (being poor/living with barely enough to get by, or at least less than those we associate with) will display our humble Christian walk.
^ We may reason that a *survival mentality* (fighting to just stay alive, or constantly living 'under-attack') will show that we are not spiritually arrogant or intimidating to others.
^ An *escape mentality* (living for the moment we get to escape this trial called earth) may get us out of the responsibility of

making a difference today because there may not be a tomorrow. We may hope that Jesus will return sooner than later, and that all our problems will then disappear, as we will be safe and sound in heaven.

Kingdom lifestyle is about demonstrating the authority of the Lord Jesus Christ, so that we can impact the world both now, and into the future.

Romans 5:17 For if by one^ man's offense death reigned through the one, much more* those who receive abundance of grace and of the gift of righteousness will reign in life through the One, Jesus Christ.

^ The sin of this one man, Adam, caused death to be king over all. (Tay)

* To a much greater degree will those who continue to receive the overflow of His unmerited favor and His gift of right standing with Himself, reign in real life through one, Jesus Christ. (Wms)

* Far more shall the reign of life be established in those who receive the overflowing fullness of the free gift of righteousness by the one man Jesus Christ. (Con)

Adam's dominion in Eden was perfect before the fall, and the church is called to return to a similar position of perfection in the end. This scripture compares the dominion that death has obtained over Adam, with the dominion that life should have through the church. Because of sin, the sting of death was severe, cold, and relentless. Death took a hold of Adam, and ended his paradise reign forever.

The free gift of salvation and righteousness then came through Jesus Christ. The tables were turned through the last Adam. Jesus came to give life to all mankind. His grace and favor were given in unlimited measure when Jesus died on the cross and rose from the dead. He took back the keys of the kingdom and was seated at the right hand of the Father in His rightful place of authority. We are in Him, and because of our connection, we can now reign from a position that is much higher, and far more wonderful. This perfect reign will be established through those who receive His amazing grace in the kingdom of God.

———————————————

Ephesians 1:3 Blessed be the God and Father of our Lord Jesus Christ, who has blessed us with every spiritual blessing in the heavenly places in Christ.

We are blessed. No demon can curse those whom God has blessed. Kingdom lifestyle means talking about the goodness of God, as well as walking in His incredible blessings.

Ephesians 1:4 He chose us in Him before the foundation of the world, that we should be holy and without blame before Him* in love.

* To be consecrated and above reproach in His sight in love. (Gsp)

We are chosen. We have a mandate on the earth that was given to us in Christ before the foundation of the earth. We are not the chosen few, but the chosen multitude that include all generations. We are chosen for greatness in the earth.

Ephesians 1:5 Having predestined us to adoption as sons by Jesus Christ to Himself, according to the good pleasure of His will.

We are adopted, not illegitimate. We are the children of the Most High God, with all of the legal privileges and responsibilities that come with being true sons and daughters.

KINGDOM AUTHORITY

Ephesians 1:6 To the praise of the glory of His grace, by which He made us accepted in the Beloved.

We are accepted, not rejected. God hasn't made a mistake allowing us to slip through the door into His family. We are members of the household of God. A great cloud of witnesses surrounds us; we are God's special people— part of a family that spans generations.

Ephesians 1:7 In Him we have redemption through His blood, the forgiveness of sins, according to the riches of His grace.

We are forgiven and reconciled to God through his amazing mercy outworked through Jesus for the salvation of all men. God lovingly delivered our souls from the pit of corruption. He has cast all our sins behind His back. *(Isa 38:17a)* We are not sinners anymore, but forgiven sons and daughters of the Most High God. The phrase: 'I am just a sinner' is no longer an excuse to be ignorant and passive. It is no longer a reason for our good intentions to turn into dancing with the devil. We are forgiven sinners and we should have zero tolerance for sin in any form or shape. We can now bring healing and forgiveness to a wicked generation. We are living in the kingdom reality of God's amazing grace.

Ephesians 1:11a In Him also we have obtained an inheritance.

We have obtained an incredible inheritance. We are wealthy citizens of heaven and heirs of righteousness. The Son of God died on a cross, and we became beneficiaries of God's eternal riches- right here and now! This kingdom reality is a lifestyle and not a futuristic fantasy.

Ephesians 1:17 That the God of our Lord Jesus Christ, the Father of glory, may give to you the spirit of wisdom and revelation in the knowledge of Him.

We have received the spirit of wisdom and revelation. We make accurate decisions as we pursue the kingdom lifestyle. We learn from our mistakes and we follow the Holy Spirit's call in everything we do. *We thrive on fresh revelation from the throne room of heaven.*

Ephesians 1:18 The eyes of your understanding being enlightened; that you may know what is the hope of His calling.

We have understanding. We are enlightened, in the true sense, because we walk in the Light. Darkness cannot prevail in the kingdom of light and truth. God has called us out of darkness and we are now living in the light of His amazing kingdom domain.

Acts 17:26 And He has made from one blood every nation of men to dwell on all the face of the earth, and has determined their pre-appointed times and the boundaries of their dwellings.

God placed us on the earth at a specific time and for an explicit purpose. We were born in the exact city and country that God has determined for us. God hand-picked our current location of work, school or university. He knows our names and addresses, and every intimate detail of our lives. The good thing is that He's not coming to 'get us' or to punish us, but He desires habitation with His own people. He has already called us and is calling us right now. He wants us to be a part of His plans and He needs us to choose to come on board. Of course God can do anything without you and me, but He wants to include us in the adventure so we can share in the joy of it.

God decided to plant us in the earth, and in this particular time, for a greater reason. You are living in the city where God wants you to live right now. You work at the exact place where He wants you to be so that you can influence specific people. You are in the school, college, and church where God wants you to be at this very moment. Although you may currently experience feelings of frustration and discomfort, remember that God has pre-appointed your times and dwellings. He never makes a mistake. *You are chosen for greatness.*

4

SPIRITUAL AUTHORITY

Let us start this chapter by examining two scenarios set in busy traffic.

Scenario 1

Imagine a young woman dressed in jeans and a T-shirt trying to stop a huge semi-trailer in the middle of a busy highway. There is no obvious emergency when the lady runs unto the highway shouting and waving her arms to convince the driver to stop his truck. What are the chances of the driver stopping if she is not directly in his path?

Scenario 2

Imagine the same woman, this time dressed not in Jeans and a T-shirt, but in a police uniform. All she needs to do is use her delegated authority as an officer of the law and raise her hand to tell the driver of the truck to stop.

The second example shows the power of authority to transform a seemingly insignificant person into a person with power. Her uniform represents a higher authority structure. As an officer of the law, this lady takes this action, knowing that she has the legal support of the entire country's police force behind her. She can step into the middle of the highway, convinced that the semi-trailer will stop because of the formidable influence she represents.

The only way any person can walk onto the highway and have a positive result is by qualifying at the police training facility as a police officer, and being released by their superiors to enforce their corporate duty.

1 John 4:17b As He is, so are we in this world.

Jesus Christ has the ultimate power and is the supreme authority over all things. We represent Jesus Christ on the earth; we are like Him; we have the mind of Christ and as He reigns supreme, so do we. He wants all people to come to Him, so do we. He wants all nations to accept His sovereign rule, so do we. He has all authority, so do we. He has delegated this power to us and we now have the spiritual authority to stop demonic forces in their tracks in the name of Jesus Christ. We can heal the sick, bless the governments of this world and bring salvation to all the nations on the earth in the name of Jesus Christ. *We are in this world to change this world. We have the real force behind us.*

The Bible tells us about the seven sons of Sceva, a Jewish priest, who learned a lesson about spiritual authority the hard way. These young men decided to cast out evil spirits from people by the authority of the Jesus that Paul preached, because they had seen or heard about the success that Paul was experiencing doing it that way. The problem was that they tried to copy the miracles that Paul performed without understanding the reason behind Paul's success, namely that He was in relationship with Jesus Christ.

In response to their attempted exorcism, a demon asked them a fair question: 'Jesus I know, and Paul I know; but who are you?' I can just imagine their shock and disbelief when the evil spirit refused to obey their demands. The demon knew that these seven blokes were not connected to the power source and proceeded to overpower them, giving them a good beating. They fled the house naked, wounded, and very confused. *(Acts 19:13-16)*

The kingdom life is neither a game nor some religious methodology. We have received our spiritual authority from the King of heaven and earth, Jesus Christ. All the forces of heaven support us when we speak. We have nothing to fear. We represent God and heaven. Demons scatter when we speak.

We have a choice of operating from a performance mindset like the sons of Sceva, or actually living in kingdom power because of our position in Jesus Christ, the Son of God.

———————————

Philippians 2:9-11 Therefore God also has highly exalted^ Him and given Him the name which is above every name, * that at the name of Jesus every knee should bow, of those in heaven, and of those on earth, and of those under the earth, and that every tongue should confess that Jesus Christ is Lord.

^ And that is why God has raised Him to the very highest place. (TCNT)
* And has conferred on Him the Name which is supreme above every other name. (Wey)

Matthew 28:18 All authority^ has been given to Me in heaven and on earth.
^ All authority [all power of rule]. (Amp)
^ Full authority has been committed to me. (NEB)

When provoked, injured, mistreated or humiliated, people often verbally abuse the name of Jesus Christ. In moments of extreme fear, many people have called out to God or to Jesus Christ. In all my life I've never heard anyone calling out to Krishna, Buddha, or to the President of his country for that matter. The reality is that even though people may not believe in Jesus Christ, they find themselves calling out to Him. Although people don't use His name with respect in many situations, it does point to the fact that there is no other name that carries such high recognition. It really is the name on everybody's lips.

Every person in heaven and on earth will declare His name as the name above all names. The Father has given a position of authority to the Son— He rules over everything. The name of Jesus Christ represents absolute supremacy over all people, governments, constellations, and realms. *The name of the Lord Jesus Christ will be acknowledged, proclaimed, honoured and worshipped in all the continents on planet earth, and in the heavens beyond.*

*Colossians 2:9,10 For in Him dwells all the fullness of the Godhead bodily; and you are complete in Him, who is the head of all principality and power. **

* Who is the authority over all authorities, and the supreme power over all powers. (Phi)
* For in Christ there is all of God in a human body; so you have everything when you have Christ, and you are filled with God through your union with Christ; He is the highest ruler over every other power. (Tay)

Colossians 2:15 Having disarmed principalities and powers, He made a public spectacle of them, triumphing* over them in it.

* And put them to open shame, leading them captive in the triumph of Christ. (Con)
* He exposed them, shattered, empty and defeated, in His final glorious triumphant act! (Phi)
* God disarmed the principalities and powers, in triumphing over them in Him and in it (on the cross). (Amp)

Jesus Christ didn't just die a horrific death so that we don't have to go to hell. His crucifixion had eternal ramifications in heaven and on earth. Armies of demons were defeated while the army of the Lord has received spiritual authority to reign supreme forever.

The finished work of Jesus Christ on the cross, had a dual effect on the kingdom of darkness and on the kingdom of light which resulted in the following:

Kingdom of darkness:

Dangerous demons are now disarmed.

The dragon is on his wagon.

The devil fell, and is in hell.

Kingdom of light:

Because of sin we were defeated, but now we are completed.

Jesus is on the throne, and we are not alone.

Because of Him, we reign supreme!

————————————

Matthew 16:18,19 And on this rock I will build My church, and the gates of Hades shall not prevail against it. And I will give you the keys of the kingdom of heaven, and whatever you bind on earth will be bound in heaven, and whatever you loose on earth, will be loosed in heaven.

Peter acknowledged Jesus as the Christ. We all need to have the same revelation. Jesus is the anointed Messiah, the Son of the living God who created the majestic mountains as well as the microscopic wonders on the face of the earth. Peter identified Jesus as the Christ because of his relationship with God himself. Some called Jesus Elijah, and others called Him

Jeremiah and even John the Baptist. Peter wasn't influenced by the popular voices of his time, or by the opinions of others.

Peter's understanding of who Jesus is transferred him into a dimension of authority and power. *He wasn't super-spiritual, but he wasn't ignorant either. He knew what he felt in his innermost being. He knew that Jesus is the Christ of God.*

Matthew 10:1 He gave them power over unclean spirits, to cast them out, and to heal all kinds of disease.

1 Corinthians 6:2 It is God's people who are to judge (manage) the world; surely you know that! (NEB)

1 Corinthians 6:3 Do you not know that we shall judge angels? How much more, things that pertain to this life? *

* How much more, then, of these matters of every day life? (Nor)

We possess heavenly authority. We have the keys to open and to close spiritual doors. We have received heaven's approval to live in the supernatural dimension of God's kingdom. We penetrate dark domains with the light of God. We heal the sick and cast out demonic forces from our homes, communities, cities, and countries.

———————

Ephesians 6:11 Put on the whole armor of God that you may be able to stand against the wiles of the devil.

Ephesians 6:13, 14a Therefore take up the whole armor of God that you may be able to withstand in the evil day, and having done all, to stand. Stand therefore.

The armor of God, as described in these verses, is for displaying power and demonstrating authority. We are the army of God and we represent the weight of heaven's glory. We stand complete in God. The battle is conquered, the war is

finished, and the fight has ended in victory. The kingdom of God displays the supremacy and superiority of God and His people over all demons, devils, evil, and dark   powers. We are clearly directed to position ourselves in this life with the authority of royal soldiers in the army of God, and to stand.

As the army of God we are exclusively assigned to fight the good fight of faith. *(1 Timothy 6:12)* God's kingdom is forcefully advancing, and the gates of hell will not prevail. This clearly paints a picture of a church on the offensive, taking ground. Surely we are taking ground from the enemy. We fight with our weapon of faith, proclaiming the word of God with our mouths. We speak life over people, circumstances and places. We don't have conversations with the devil, but we rebuke him.

We talk and walk with Jesus, and He alone is our focus in every situation. We stand on solid, holy ground. We don't take a step backwards. We do not have to detect or salute evil princes over cities, and demonic rulers over countries. We follow the Commander of the army of the Lord!

Faith involves us pronouncing Jesus Christ as the King over all the earth. Jesus never had conversations with demons. He basically told them to shut up! He never told us to investigate the ancestry of demons, discuss their locality and influence, or give them any credit at all. Jesus cast them out and He wants us to do the same. *Our fight is a good one; it is a journey of faith.*

Ephesians 14b-18a Having girded your waist with truth, having put on the breastplate of righteousness, and having shod your feet with the preparation of the gospel of peace; above all, taking the shield of faith with which you will be able to quench all the fiery darts of the wicked one. And take the helmet of salvation, and the sword of Spirit, which is the word of God; praying always with all prayer and supplication in the Spirit.

These verses give us a clear understanding of the armory we possess as we pursue our battle formation.

Let me explain the function of the armor in textbook style:

The Girdle of Truth.

The belt of truth around the waist keeps your armor in position. This speaks about how necessary it is to bring balance to our lives. It connects all the other parts, and brings them to a position of stability and readiness for battle. Jesus Christ is the truth. He sets us free. He is the epicenter of our lives. He is the true King of the kingdom.

The Breastplate of Righteousness.

The breastplate of righteousness covers your heart from evil attacks, offenses, and shame. We have received an amazing heavenly heart transplant, and we should protect and keep our new hearts pure. Jesus Christ is our righteousness; He has made us right with God.

The Shoes of Preparation of the Gospel of Peace.

The shoes protect your feet and will keep you moving forward. By proclaiming the word of God consistently, we advance the kingdom daily. The shoes reflect our willingness to take ground for God, and to shamelessly declare the gospel of peace. Jesus Christ is the Prince of peace, and we are His peacemakers. We walk in His footsteps, prepared and ready to preach the gospel of peace.

The Shield of Faith.

The shield of faith protects you from the enemy's fiery

attacks. His arrows of fear, hate, unforgiveness, poverty, violence, and jealousy will not be able to penetrate the shield of faith. Faith can protect your body from sickness, your soul from emotional turmoil, and your spirit from drifting away from an awareness of the presence of God. Our vibrant faith in God activates this shield to operate on our behalf, even in the most challenging situations.

The Helmet of Salvation.

The helmet of salvation protects your mind from serious injuries. The head contains our intellect, will, ability to choose, as well as our thought patterns; and it needs the best possible protection. When our minds get invaded, our whole life can be influenced. Jesus is our mighty Savior. As the head of His body, He has great knowledge about all the possible dangers we are exposed to in our minds. There are many battles to be fought in our heads, and we need to be alert and prepared.

The Sword of the Spirit.

This is the only offensive weapon in our armory. We need to take up the sword of the Spirit, which is the word of God. We fight the good fight of faith by knowing, believing, and speaking the word of God. When we speak the word, we agree with God's own declarations about our lives. Using the sword of the Spirit, we will remain victorious in all areas of our lives.

Praying Always.

We are royal guards. We stand with authority. We are called to stand. We stand prayerfully, trusting God unconditionally. Our prayers are not weak and hopeless utterances, but powerful proclamations that make demons tremble and evil kingdoms fall. We wear the full armor of God every day and every night—it is our lifestyle.

KINGDOM AUTHORITY

We don't use the armor of God to pick a fight with the devil. We don't take the armor off to rest, either. We work, play, pray and live fully armored and prepared for anything. We speak life, walk in integrity, believe God, preach the gospel,

and pray constantly. We stand with authority and we reign in this life because of the finished work of our Lord Jesus Christ.

5

THE BEST IS YET TO COME

No one walks into a new place backwards, yet many Christians walk through life looking to the past, either with longing for the way things were, or with regret for the things that have been. When we talk about and dwell on our past failures and sins, we invite principalities of darkness into our world, and this is when we can become cynical, destructive and depressed. Living in the past can result into a lifestyle of regret, frustration, and spiritual lethargy. It brings about a decline in our faith level and a distortion in our relationship with God. We see darkness and live in fear instead of seeing light and living with anticipation for the break of a new day.

Genesis 19 illustrates this beautifully with the story of Lot and his family who were surrounded by godless and wicked people in the City of Sodom. The city and all its inhabitants were condemned to destruction, but because of the intercession of his uncle Abraham, Lot and his family were given a chance to escape. The angelic command was for them to flee the city, and to rush straight to the mountains for safety. (Without looking back at the city) But Lot's wife turned around to look at the city, and was changed into a pillar of salt. She was looking back at the past, to what was familiar, rather than to the future God was giving them.

Luke 9:62 No one, having put his hand to the plough, and looking back,* is fit for the kingdom of God.

* And then keeps looking back. (NEB)
* And looks back [to the things behind]. (Amp)

God's desire for us is to run through the valleys, climb over the mountains, swim across the oceans, and soar like the eagles above the high stormy clouds. *When we entertain the past, we lose focus of the future that He has for us and we begin to dwell in a place of false security- a place of familiarity with the way things were. When we look back like this, we are not able to take ground for the kingdom of God.*
We should rather call the things that do not exist as if it already exists. *(Romans 4:17)* We trust God, we believe God, and we live a life of faith. Believe it- the best is yet to come.

Jeremiah 29:11 For I know the thoughts that I think towards you, says the Lord, thoughts of peace and not of evil, to give you a future and a hope. *

* I have not lost sight of my plan for you, the Lord says, and it is your welfare I have in mind, not your undoing: for you, too, I have a destiny and a hope. (Knox)
* Plans for peace, not disaster, reserving a future full of hope for you. (Jerus)
* Thoughts and plans for welfare and peace and not for evil, to give you hope in your final outcome. (Amp)
* Prosperity and not misfortune, and a long line of children after you. (NEB)

The phrase, 'a long line of children' speaks of generational blessings. God has amazing plans for us today, as well as for our children and the generations to follow. Each is
46

a personal and amazing plan for our individual lives, but they will also have ramifications for the generations to follow. God is with us here and now. We don't have to worry about tomorrow, but we can still build towards making it a better future for our descendants. By living in what God has for us today, we invest into a better, more hopeful future for the generations to follow!

I am so thankful to witness my own children's walk with God. I just know that they will accomplish much more in this life than we have as their parents. We have loved them and we have installed the fundamentals of the kingdom of God in their lives. We are not perfect parents but God will send His rain on the good seed we have sown in their lives, and He will bring about a mighty harvest. Our children will walk where we could never have walked.

As Christians, our children will become the preachers, lawyers, politicians, teachers and business people that will establish the kingdom of God in the earth in a way that we can never imagine. They don't have to convince us that they will reach further, fly higher, run faster, and preach better- because they will. My two children are already young adults and there isn't much we can teach them now. All we can do as parents now is to direct them, pray for them, and release them into a greater future.

Jesus invested three years of His life in the lives of twelve ordinary people. They, in turn, became disciples of Jesus Christ, who influenced nations. I had the privilege over the last seven years to teach and disciple a new group of students each year. What a challenge, and yet what an opportunity! Investing every spiritual gift that is on my world into the lives of these young people, may contribute to the rising of a generation of powerful believers. They may become the next generation who can do the impossible.

We have to believe in the younger generation and teach them everything we know. They want to learn and they desire to do great things for God. We need to teach them kingdom truth and not outdated Sunday school lessons. We need to direct them on the pathway of kingdom victory and not the 'Ten Rules' of God. Young people don't want to hear what they cannot do, but what they actually can do.

We can teach the next generation about the great future that God has planned for them and that the best is yet to come. Our future and the future of our children are in God's hands, but He has given us the privilege of partnering with Him in making it happen. As we step into tomorrow, the God of our future will again be our present help. He is the God of the 'now'.

Psalms 46:1 declares that God is a very present help in our times of trouble and need. Jesus clearly teaches us that tomorrow can worry about itself. To get stressed about the future will drain your energy. Prosperity, peace and goodness are awaiting us in the future. We don't fantasise about the future by running after materialistic things or even chasing wild impossibilities. We don't play God for one moment by thinking we are immune against any bad thing. But, neither do we linger in the past.

Isaiah 38:17b For You have cast all my sins behind Your back.

God does not look back. He is not a God of the past. Our sins are cast into the depths of the sea. They are gone. The past is an evil snare that would like to capture us with its emotional temptation. *The past is past tense and the best is yet to come.*

———————————————

I truly thank God for so many memorials in my own life, as well as in the lives of others. I think of a young Sudanese refugee, Lopez Lomong who was abducted as a six-year-old boy and taken to a rebel army camp to be trained as a child soldier. In the midst of trouble and pain, Lopez had a dream to become a United States Olympian, and this is exactly what he did.

Instead of complaining about our past, present, or future, we should dream and dream again. Camping in the past- either at our successes or our failures- will prevent us from clearly looking where we are going. *We are currently building memorials for the generations that will follow us on the kingdom pathway of life.*

Lopez could see himself running on the track in an Olympic stadium. For years he had no money, family or any hope. His trust in God never faded and he started running every day, just to forget about the hunger pains, and to focus on the hope of a new tomorrow. We have to do what we can do with what we have right now. Our current condition may not be superb at the moment, but God is watching over us.

The late Mr Nelson Mandela had to persevere the trials of imprisonment, racial abuse, and isolation for twenty-seven years. Soon after his emotional release from jail, he became the President of his country. Amazing! Today, the name of Mr Nelson Mandela is renowned globally. This man stood for what he believed in, preached a life message of peace and reconciliation, and changed the lives of millions of people.

God will turn our horrible past or present into amazing stories of victory and fame. *We may be prisoners of shame, anger and unforgiveness, but we will become legendary people as we reveal the glory of God in the earth.* Our circumstances may seem totally insignificant at the moment, but God is working behind the scenes to turn it into books still to be written. Our stories will one day be told and many lives will be influenced.

*Philippians 1:6 Being confident of this very thing, that He who has begun a good work in you will complete it * until the day of Jesus Christ.*

* Developing [that good work] and perfecting and bringing it to full completion in you. (Amp)

* Will bring it to completion by the day. (NEB)

God has begun a good work in all of us. This is the starting point. We all have a talent or a gift that we have received from God. We have to believe and embrace this fact. God released these gifts into our lives so that we can influence the world, and bring Him glory. We are saved and called for a reason. The wonderful reality is that God has promised to complete, fulfill, and perfect His work in us until the day of Jesus Christ.

This process is continuous; it is progressive. We don't want to look back one day and wonder with regret what happened with our lives, and where we have missed the boat. We should rather be thanking God for the things he has initiated in our lives, and run the race with perseverance towards the finishing line, knowing He runs with us.

*Hebrews 6:1 Therefore, leaving the discussions of the elementary principles of Christ, let us go on to perfection.**

* And continue progressing toward maturity. (Wms)
* Therefore let us go on and get past the elementary stage in the teachings and doctrines of Christ, advancing steadily toward the completeness and perfection that belong to spiritual maturity. (Amp)
* And pass on to our full growth. (Knox)

The kingdom of God is not made up of people who are perfect, but people who are striving towards perfection. Our goal on earth is to pursue our kingdom mandate of bringing perfection into an imperfect world. Perfection is our target- this is why we pray that His kingdom will come on earth as it is in heaven. If we are not aiming for this, we are

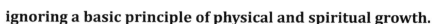

ignoring a basic principle of physical and spiritual growth.

God wants us, His people, to reach maturity in Christ. We have to aim for the stars so that we can reach beyond our limited range. *We are not perfect, but we do not focus on our restrictions, we focus on His limitlessness. We may yet be far away, but we are to be on our way to perfection.*

John 10:10 The thief does not come except to steal, and to kill, and to destroy. I have come that they may have life, and that they may have it more abundantly.*

* And have it overflowing in them. (Beck)
* And enjoy life, and have it in abundance [to the full, till it overflows]. (Amp)

Jesus came to give us a great life. He doesn't want us just to go through the motions, trapped in repetitive routines. We sometimes focus to much on our frustrations, needs and desires, and we lose perspective. We actually struggle to visualize the bigger picture when we allow the challenges and problems we encounter to overwhelm us.

There is a thief who would like to destroy your life through sickness, stress, relationship issues, financial problems, spiritual legalism or apathy. Whatever purposeful enterprise is launched against you can never have the power to kill or destroy you. No threat is strong enough to kill or eliminate you. Never give the devil any authority in your life that has not been granted to him by God. Jesus defeated him and his position is under our feet— we have authority over our enemy. *(Luke 10:19)* Nothing can stop the river of God's abundance from flowing into your life except the things you allow to stand in the way of heaven's blessings.

———————————-

Revelation 11:15- Then the seventh angel sounded: And there *were loud voices in heaven, saying, 'The kingdoms of this world have become the kingdoms of our Lord and of His Christ,* and He shall reign forever and ever!*

* The dominion, [kingdom, sovereignty, rule] of the world has now come into the possession of our Lord and of His Christ. (Amp)

Jesus Christ reigned from the beginning. He is the beginning and the end. Governments will bow before Him. The entire entertainment industry, the political arena, as well as the economic forces of this world will acknowledge Him as the supreme ruler. All the kingdoms of this world will come to acknowledge Christ's sovereignty. The richest, most influential individuals and nations in the world will one day declare His dominion.

Many Christians are waiting for Christ to return so that His eternal reign can be announced. But Christ's supreme rule has already been announced, and only has to be revealed and outworked on earth as it is in heaven. We need to believe the word of God as it is   revealed. We need to proclaim the truth. Christ is the ruler, and the church can implement this victory today.

Some Christians believe that Christ and His kingdom's reign are only futuristic. This concept robs the church of the opportunity to live in victory right now. We need to understand that our God is a God of the present. He has anointed us to declare His majesty to this world right now. We don't need to wait for something to happen— it already did, at Calvary, two thousand years ago. The kingdom of God is within us, and we can utilize this perfect power inside of us to turn this world the right side up. *(Luke 17:20,21).*

This kingdom is not a physical kingdom, but a spiritual realm. There is no constitution to be formed, president to be voted for, or any other form of governmental action that can be performed to establish this kingdom. It is invisible and invincible, yet tangible and real.

This kingdom is impenetrable and indestructible. It cannot be restricted to any single place or time. It is everywhere and always there.

We are establishing the kingdom reality where we live or work, when we are on holidays, and when we have a meal with friends or family. It is ever existing, ever progressing and everlasting. The church should take advantage of the power that has been imparted to us by applying the kingdom in this world. We need to infiltrate society with the love of God, through faith and prayer. We need to demonstrate this kingdom with power, signs, and wonders. We need to celebrate the supreme reign of Christ in the earth today. Now is the time. Today is the day of the salvation and the supreme reign of our Lord.

We have been conditioned through inaccurate preaching that we will actually escape our responsibility of ultimately taking complete charge of the earth. Wrong interpretations about the future of the church, as well as distorted doctrines about the end times, paralyze the church from making an impact now. The heart of the kingdom of God is grace, peace and multiplication. Our God will give us the required strategies to endure the most difficult circumstances. We are here to take over. The best is yet to come.

We will not escape the tests and trials of life as these things are used by God to help us mature into new levels of effectiveness in the kingdom. David faced the challenge of an enormous giant in his world. For many Christians this test would have been an impossible enterprise. David accepted the challenge by faith and conquered the giant. This didn't happen because he was more anointed than anyone else, but because he had already been tested by bears and lions in the fields, and had prevailed.

This single victory against Goliath took David out of obscurity and made him a force to be reckoned with among the nations. He became a mighty man of war and led many armies to countless victories in his life. Whatever we experience now will lift us to a higher level. Whatever we have now, will multiply and accumulate in the future. God's kingdom is always growing and cannot be destroyed.

————————-

Daniel wonderfully describes the sovereign rule of the kingdom of God. These scriptures are inspirational prophetic utterances describing the powerful kingdom of God. Contrary to many popular opinions about destruction and devastation regarding the future of the church, Daniel envisions a glorious future for God's people.

Daniel 2:44 The God of heaven will set up a kingdom which shall never be destroyed; and the kingdom shall not be left to other people; it shall brake in pieces and consume all these kingdoms, and it shall stand forever.

Daniel 4:3 His kingdom is an everlasting kingdom, and His dominion is from generation to generation.

Daniel 6:26 For He is the living God, and steadfast forever; His kingdom is the one which shall not be destroyed, and His dominion shall endure to the end.

Daniel 7:14 Then to Him was given dominion and glory and a kingdom, that all peoples, nations, and languages should serve Him.

Daniel 7:18 But the saints of the Most High shall receive the kingdom, and possess the kingdom forever, even forever and ever.

Daniel 7:22 A judgment was made in favor of the saints of the Most High, and the time came for the saints to possess the kingdom.

Daniel 7:27 Then the kingdom and dominion, and the greatness of the kingdoms under the whole heaven, shall be given to the people, the saints of the Most High. His kingdom is an everlasting kingdom, and all dominions shall serve and obey Him.

Hebrews 12:28 Therefore, since we are receiving a kingdom* which cannot be shaken, let us have grace, by which we may serve God acceptably with reverence and godly fear.

* A kingdom, which will never be moved. (Bas)
* A kingdom nothing can destroy. (Tay)
* A kingdom that is firm and stable and cannot be shaken. (Amp)
* We are receiving possession. (Rhm)

By receiving the incredible kingdom of God, we are now empowered to live effective, influential, and powerful lives for God. Now is the time for us to realize that we are partakers of this unparalleled and indestructible kingdom. *We are powerful kingdom warriors, not meek and mild church folk who just try to make ends meet. We are immortal enforcers, appointed by the King of heaven to establish His supernatural kingdom on the earth.* We are not to be intimidated by any other power, but we are assigned to launch influential outpourings of love and grace into the kingdoms of this world.

Our faith should constantly remind us of the fact that these kingdoms already belong to the Lord Jesus Christ. We are not to doubt our kingdom strength. The task we are assigned to is attainable—we are not designed to be losers. We are here to take ground for God and to push back the forces of darkness slowly but surely. We have received the revelation of God's grace. He has declared us to be more than conquerors.

We need to believe and live in the reality of who we are in Christ.

KINGDOM AUTHORITY

We are peacemakers, but we are not to compromise our beliefs. We should love sinners, but we cannot tolerate sin. We are to be gentle and kind with people who are created in the image of God, but when we speak, demons ought to flee for their lives. Yes, we should turn the other cheek, but the one who should turn and run, is the devil. The Church has not always walked with confidence in our anointing to bring the kingdom of God to earth, and we may still have a way to go, but every day we work towards this perfection.

Truly, the best is yet to come!

6

THE WORD OF GOD

As mentioned in the opening chapter; I came to Christ as a nineteen-year old student in my University City, Potchefstroom, in the North West Province of the Republic of South Africa. Although I grew up in a Christian home and spend many years in Sunday school, I only fell in love with the word of God soon after my commitment to Christ. I remember how I carried a little New Testament Bible in my pocket when I served in the army. I read the Bible daily. I had memorized verses, and continuously quoted scriptures to my mates.

It wasn't long after these years that I have received opportunities to preach as a youth leader in the local Pentecostal church. Since then I have always been passionate about the word of God. I've been buying new Bibles, underlining scriptures, making 'topic- chains', writing notes, highlighting passages, memorizing scriptures and preparing sermons ever since.

My passion for the word of God originated from a real relationship with Jesus Christ. This desire to know Jesus more, to draw closer to Him and to become more intimately acquainted with Him, resulted in my daily discipline of reading the Bible. To me, reading the Bible never feels like a task, a burden or a spiritual obligation. To spend time in the word of God is a   privilege and it is a fantastic opportunity to hear the voice of God.

Regular Bible-reading confirms the reality of my relationship with my heavenly father. It involves a friend taking time out to listen to a friend. It is a crucial manner of commencing your daily routines. It is fitting to open heaven's textbook and to receive encouragement, direction, confirmation, assignments, and clarification about life's challenges on a daily basis. *If we say we love Jesus, we ought to love the word of God.*

2 Tim 3:16 All Scripture is given by inspiration of God, and is profitable for doctrine, for reproof, for correction, for instruction in righteousness.

Every scripture is God-breathed. The Bible is the word of God. It is the weight of God in our lives. It is God's instruction manual for His people. It is the gentle whisper of the Holy Spirit in our hearts. As we open the Word of God, He touches our spirit, soul and body with healing, strength, comfort, clarity, direction, and loads of loving affirmation.

Jesus Christ is the *Word* that became flesh. He has always been there and never left the heavenly realm; until the day the world desperately needed redemption. The *Word* became flesh and He was forever transformed into something tangible and real; a revealed truth and a manifested grace. *(John 1:1-14)*

Jesus Christ is my reality. He understands my body, soul, and spirit dimensions. He understands how I feel, and He knows my heart's desires. He became a human being and therefore He can relate to all my personal issues. Jesus Christ breathes over me as I am typing on my computer right now. He breathes over me when I work, play, or relax. He breathes over me when I am in dire straits about life's demands. When He breathes over me, I receive His truth and grace. This can happen constantly as we read, quote, or just meditate on the scriptures.

———————————-

1 Kings 22: 14 And Micaiah said: 'As the Lord lives, whatever the Lord says to me, that I will speak.'

Jehoshaphat, the king of Judah decided to inquire of the Lord before he went into battle. This was an excellent decision as it could have determined a future of life or death for the entire nation. The words that Micaiah spoke were not the most applauded in this time, and the popular prophets of the day vigorously opposed his message. But he was a man of integrity who refused to be controlled by any human authority. His honesty and boldness brought him imprisonment through the king of Israel, but his words spoke in the end. The battle increased, and this king died on that same day.

We are the Micaiahs of the Lord in the earth today. We may never be popular, but we have to be faithful to God. We may be intimidated, but we will not be silenced. God's message may not be popular everywhere, but it still needs to be declared.

Present day prophets may have a selection of opinions, but we need to declare the word of our God in all circumstances. People may prefer to listen to well-designed lectures and soothing prophecies, but the word of the Lord will speak in the end. And the word is undeniably going to speak through the people of God.

Nobody sets out to eat a huge meal never to eat again. Hunger comes back at you at regular intervals. We need to have an intense hunger for the food that heaven provides. I watched a news bulletin recently about a pastor who said that he is going to function without God for an entire year-shocking! I would never want to live without God; not even for a moment.

People who go on a hunger strike can only remain alive for a certain amount of days. The lack of spiritual food will bring death to our spirit being. Death may come slowly, but it will come.

Israel received fresh manna from heaven on a daily basis. The manna from the previous day was inedible. It works exactly the same in our spiritual walk with God. We have to eat food every day, and we have to read God's word every day!

Hebrews 4:12 For the word of God* is living and powerful, and sharper than any two-edged sword, piercing even to the division of soul and spirit, and of joints and marrow, and is a discerner of the thoughts and intents of the heart.

* For the word of God is living, and active. (ASV)
* For the word of God is full of life and power. (Wey)
* For the word of God is quick, and powerful. (KJV)
* For living is the word of God and energetic. (Rhm)
* For the Word that God speaks is alive and full of power [making it active, operative, energizing, and effective]. (Amp)

Words are very important in everyday life. There are words of love and affirmation. There are words of manipulation and antagonism. The declarations that our parents and teachers spoke over our lives were words of either life or death. Words have the power to either shape us or break us. The most important affirmations that can be spoken over our worlds come from the matchless word of God.

The Bible is not just another good book. It encapsulates the plans and purposes of God for our lives. It reveals heaven's destiny and prosperity for our cities. It releases the healing power of God to the hurt and broken people in our streets. It brings kingdom truth, fresh revelation knowledge, and Holy Spirit power to our churches and families.

I just love to buy new Bibles. I read and keep on reading. This is the only book with no real beginning and end. It continuously captures my attention. Although it is so easy for me to fall asleep during an action–packed movie, I have never fallen asleep while reading the Bible. I find new passion and energy when I read and share the scriptures.

The same Bible verse can bring a diversity of meanings and solutions to people of all nations and languages at exactly the same moment. There is no confusion in that, because the Holy Spirit operates smartly. God knows what He is saying and what people need to hear in the perfect moment.

Colossians 2:6 As you therefore have received Christ Jesus the Lord, so walk in Him.

We have received Christ as the word from heaven. We should respond by living according to the word and by living in the word. I am not referring to the preoccupation of memorizing scriptures, and being religious about it. I am talking about becoming more like Jesus; operating in the reality of the written word. I am talking about a natural, easy, sweet walk with Christ. Loving the word of God is a huge part of this wonderful journey.

———————————

In the *Gospel of Matthew* we read about Jesus being tempted by the devil for forty days.

He was tempted in the area of the flesh (The physical body):

This is a common area wherein our enemy will try his utmost best to destroy us. We will mostly be tempted with fleshly desires in the area of sex, finances or pride. The devil

61

wanted Jesus to fail after His long fast, provoking Him into turning some stones into bread. Jesus realized that this was an ambush from the enemy and responded by quoting this scripture:

Matthew 4:4 Man shall not live by bread alone, but by every word that proceeds from the mouth of God.

Although Jesus was tempted during the full extent of forty days, the attack from the devil advanced to its most vigorous stage towards the very end. We now know that the devil's strategy would be to launch a forceful assault on us when we are physically at our weakest. Imagine how weak Jesus was after not eating any food for forty days. Even when we are physically weak, we have to be spiritually strong and vigilant. We need to know the Bible well enough to be able to quote accurate scriptures at any time and in any required situation.

Not being able to quote scriptures accurately, may lead to some serious spiritual battle scars. If we find ourselves in a similar situation like Jesus, it will be extremely beneficial to know some Bible scriptures. Even if you just recently started your journey with God, it would be good to have a passion to absorb some basic scriptures as soon as possible. This is how we grow. This is how we conquer.

Although the devil is conquered by Christ and alleged to be under our feet, we may still be tempted, tested, or challenged by our old adversary. In difficult spiritual situations like this, it can be too late to fast, pray, or to call the pastor. The temptation could occur the very moment when we would have to resist the devil by quoting relevant and accurate scriptures. Displaying our spiritual authority like Jesus will confuse the enemy and he will think twice before challenging us again.

He was tempted in the area of the soul dimension (The mind):

This is a common area where the devil will consistently try to terrorize the people of God. He employs strategies of targeting our mindsets and thought patterns with negativity, confusion, and depression. We have to effectively and deliberately counterattack his strategies.

Satan tried to deviously mislead Jesus into a thought process that could have been suicidal and destructive. He ultimately wanted Jesus to jump off the temple tower to fall to His death. The devil even quoted a scripture out of context when he reminded Jesus that the angels would catch Him if He falls. Thankfully, Jesus was alert to this devious and cunning attack, and responded again by quoting the proceeding word of God:

Matthew 4:7 You shall not tempt the Lord your God.

He was tempted in the spiritual realm (The heart):

As the father of all lies, the devil will do anything to be acknowledged. He took Jesus to a high mountain where he pursued the most arrogant, rebellious, and blasphemous attack that has ever been recorded. Satan essentially desired to be God. He sought to be the king of all the high places; to be the ruler of all kingdoms. He craved worship. Satan offered Jesus all the kingdoms of this world as if it all belonged to him. He knew how much he would gain if he could persuade the Son of God to worship him. This arrogance has displayed the full extend of the distortion of the devil's mind. Jesus once again responded by proclaiming this powerful and accurate scripture:

Matthew 4:10 Away with you Satan! For it is written, 'You shall worship the Lord your God, and Him only you shall serve.'

63

KINGDOM AUTHORITY

Our mandate is to be constantly alert in the areas of relationship, art and culture, sport and recreation, politics and comedy, as well as economy, finances and music. The word of God is superior to any situation, kingdom, individual, or government. We will be unswervingly victorious by believing and proclaiming the proceeding, manifested word of the Lord every day, as we worship God alone.

———————————-

2 Timothy 4:1-4 I charge you therefore before God and the Lord Jesus Christ, who will judge the living and the dead at His appearing and His kingdom; Preach the word!* Be ready in season and out of season. Convince, rebuke, exhort, with all longsuffering and teaching. For the time will come^ when they will not endure sound doctrine, but according to their own desires, because they have itching ears, they will heap up for themselves teachers; and they will turn their ears away from the truth, and be turned aside to fables.

* Preach the word; be ready in season and out of season; reprove, rebuke, and exhort, with complete patience and teaching. For the time is coming when people will not endure sound teaching, but having itching ears they will accumulate for themselves teachers to suit their own passions, and will turn away from listening to the truth and wander off into myths. (ESV)
* Preach the word; press it home on all occasions, convenient or inconvenient. (NEB)
* Be at it when it is and when it is not convenient. (Ber)
* Never lose your sense of urgency. (Phi)
* Whether the opportunity seems to be favourable or unfavourable, being unflagging and inexhaustible in patience and teaching. (Amp)
^ For the time will come when people decline to be taught sound doctrine. (Mof)

^ For there will be a season, when the healthful teaching they will not endure. (Rhm)
^ But, moved by their own desires. (Bas)
^ But to gratify their own evil desires. (Wms)
^ To satisfy their own fancies. (Wey)

The word of God should be preached accurately, relentlessly, and passionately. There is a longing in creation to hear the solid, sound and perfect word of God. There are enough novels, stories and fables out there to whisper in the itching ears of religion seekers. Paul's advice to all preachers is crystal clear: 'Preach the word, teach the word, and speak the word.' I find it absolutely alarming that pastors and preachers in our day and age can water down the significance of teaching and speaking the word of God. In this age of 'seeker sensitivity' and 'cultural correctness', church leaders are easily swayed to compromise the powerful word of the living God.

Kingdom preachers should not deliver ego-centred presentations. They should not be performing theatrical productions. They should not merely tell stories. Some sermons are delivered with little, and even without biblical content. Paul released a caution to the church about these diluted messages that will be presented in the church. Unfortunately, it is happening today. This is a demonic effort to weaken the kingdom of God, and can only be counteracted by the clear-cut preaching of the word of God.

We are currently living in incredibly significant times on the earth. I believe that passionate, Bible believing, uncompromising, kingdom-focused preachers of God's eternal word will unapologetically rise to the occasion. This is the season to take a stand with Paul, and not a time to give in to the secular demands of a contemporary church.

I am not a conservative, 'old school' person, and I love progressive transformation, modern strategies, and renewed vision; I actually dislike out-dated thinking in terms of rules and regulations in the managing of churches today. As kingdom people who love God's word, though, we have to take a stand against the idea of preaching a watered down message to accommodate seeker sensitive visitors and Holy Spirit insensitive church leaders.

We should not do Bible 'punching', or be preaching to people when they are not likely to receive the word of the Lord. It may take a long time for people's hearts to become receptive to the message of God. But the other side of the coin is also true, and equally important. According to the apostle Paul we should preach the gospel in season and out of season. I believe that instead of being super sensitive to the demands of society, we should rather be sensitive to the Holy Spirit and boldly declare the word of the Lord to all people.

I am not talking about preaching a ridiculous message of condemnation, hellfire and judgement on the street corners or behind our pulpits. I am talking about declaring the word of the Lord, just as it is. We should proclaim the gospel message of hope, salvation, and faith. We should speak the word of God. We never have to say: "Thus says the Lord!" People don't need to know we are actually quoting the Bible. All they need to know is that someone loves them. Speaking life over people will uplift their human nature. People don't have to accept Christ there and then. We just need to speak words of encouragement and peace over people.

———————————-

In the kingdom of God our prayers ought to reflect the word of God. Younger Christians may not follow your knowledge, but they will follow your example of praying the word. Praying perfect grammar phrases, or even well prepared sentences, will not make your prayer effective. The enemy of our souls will only flee if we resist him with the quoting of the scriptures. Conscientious procedures and brilliantly laid out prayer structures will not lead to any results in the kingdom.

Leaders praying immature prayers from the pulpits should be sympathetically reprimanded. Jesus Himself taught us to address the Father when we pray. Our prayers should be word- based (seeking the attention of our loving Father), and not poem-like performances (seeking the approval of people). Unbelievers are looking for authenticity, not pretence. Our children receive inaccurate examples of prayer whilst they are supposed to become our future prayer warriors.

Although unbelievers may not know much about church life, they will be able to identify phony preaching and pretentious praying immediately. They will see the masks of false holiness, righteousness, and self-ambition behind the pulpit. They will sense the judgement, criticism, or false humility in the congregation. Unbelievers come to church to hear the word of God, to see miracles, and to experience the tangible love of God. They don't come for a spectacle, a concert, or a comedy.

They come out of desperation for something supernatural. They want to hear the truth and they want to see the word of God in action.

————————————

Romans 10:8 The word* is near you, in your mouth and in your heart (that is, the word of faith^ which we preach).

* The Word (God's message in Christ) is near you, on your lips and in your heart. (Amp)
^ Which means The Message of Faith, which we proclaim. (TCNT)

Romans 10:17 So the faith comes by hearing, and hearing by the word of God.

We have to come to the understanding that we are obligated to teach and preach the word of God. Anything different in our hearts is not to be preached. Stories may sound good, but only the preaching of the word will bring freedom, growth, and authority in people's lives. We may draw a good crowd by telling fantastic stories and tales, but we will never enthuse our listeners to become people of faith.

People listening to the word of faith, will become strong in their walk of faith. The word is established in our hearts and we need to preach this word of faith. It is irresponsible conduct from church leaders to keep the people incompetent and untrained. The reason leaders do this might be a lack of self- confidence in their own spiritual capacity. It might also be spiritual pride.

These leaders will do anything to control everything in the life of the church. They feel threatened when strong spiritual men and women of God enter the church setting. Instead of utilising these gifts to the body of Christ, some leaders put them on hold forever and a day. Consequently these 'intimidating' people are regularly assigned to ministry tasks in the church that will never emphasize their gifts and calling.

These leaders actually work against the kingdom purposes of God and against Christ's instructions. They are opposing basic Bible principles of teaching and preaching and would prefer speakers on the pulpit who will be super gentle with the people. We should always love the people, but doctrinal inaccuracy cannot be dealt with casually in the *kingdom of God*. It needs to be addressed apostolically. Demonic challenges cannot be dealt with by humorous comments and easy-going confrontations. It needs to be dealt with forcefully by declaring the powerful truth of the Bible, and nothing else.

We can never activate faith in the lives of God's people the American, Australian or African way (Or even the way of a specific movement or organization). We need to operate in kingdom culture; and do things God's way!

I remember a lady coming out for prayer after my sermon one Sunday. She looked devastated, on the edge of an anxiety attack. She responded to the message with faith and hope. I then spoke two words to her with boldness and authority: "Fear, go!" She trampled a few steps backwards and fell to the ground. She later testified that she was completely set free from the bondage of fear and inferiority. I spoke only two words but these words were the word of God *(2 Timothy 1:7)*. God did not give us a spirit of fear and therefore we can declare His truth and set people free.

Medical professionals, psychiatrists, and other spiritual healers may also contribute to various degrees of healing and restoration in people's lives. Many times these contributions are just temporary. Hearing the word of God and getting your faith stirred, will bring you into the reality of the miraculous. Solutions to problems, healing of hurt, and supernatural provision in impossible situations, become real and regular. The word of God brings victory over pain, strife, and darkness. All we have to do is to hear the word of the Lord, believe it, speak it and live it!

Titus 1:2,3 In hope of eternal life which God, who cannot lie, promised before time began, but has in due time manifested His word through preaching.*

* And at the appointed time He made known his word through preaching. (Wey)
* But hath manifested in its fitting seasons, even his word through preaching. (Rhm)

It is clear that God has designed His wonderful message to be heard through *preaching*. I am a preacher and I count myself immensely privileged. People get stage fear when they have to step towards a pulpit to speak publicly. I get so excited, that I can barely wait to be introduced and start preaching. What really moves me is the message. The message is in the Book.

69

If you read your Bible as a preacher, and you have a love-relationship with God, you will never search for a message. You essentially ask God what *not* to say. *As a preacher of the word of God, you live prepared.* I remember how I stressed   myself out for days to unearth a message to preach. Those days are now long-gone. The word is in our hearts and on our lips. We should be ready to preach at any time, at any location, and on any topic.

Why would we preach out of books, or prepare messages from the Internet? We don't need the Internet and we don't need other preacher's materials, because the Bible is an ongoing message in itself. The message is in the Bible, which is the word of God. It is time for the global church to turn back to the basics- back to God's eternal drawing board. We have to teach the next generation about the power and grace of preaching the word of God.

Titus 1:9 Holding fast the faithful word as he has been taught, that he may be able, by sound doctrine, both to exhort and convict those who contradict.

By hearing the uncompromising word of God we become people who actually believe this message of faith. This is when we actually 'become able' to speak the sound word of God into any appropriate situation or challenge.

Jesus Christ is the sacrificial *Lamb* of God. He is gentle, kind and loving. The church is called to operate like the *Lamb* when it deals with all kinds of people in this world. We need to draw sinners to God through love and kindness. We could randomly buy someone a cup of coffee, offer to put away their trolley, or put air into their vehicle's tyres.

Jesus Christ is also the *Lion* of the tribe of Judah. This makes Him formidable and powerful. When it comes to sin, demonic forces and false doctrines, the church needs to roar like the *Lion.* We should love the sinners but we should counter every form of sin, lawlessness and governmental ignorance. Our responsibility is to oppose all Biblical contradictions and to declare the sound word of the Most High God in all situations. I tend to address issues that stand against the kingdom of light in my own sphere of life, and regularly find a response of either total ignorance, or judgmental reprimand. (Ignorance from sinners and reprimand from religious circles).

Titus 2:1 But as for you, speak the things which are proper for sound doctrine.

The word of God is a proceeding word. This indicates reading and hearing the word, and obeying the word of God constantly and consistently. The word of the Lord does not just come on one occasion, but continuously. It is to be desired, as we have a real relationship with a real God. God wants to speak to us daily and impact our lives continually. We cannot be content by hearing the word of the Lord occasionally at church meetings, prayer group gatherings, or yearly conferences.

Christians sometimes embrace a single word they have received from God but never progress to a higher maturity level in Christ. Hence, they live lives of frustration in the kingdom of God. They feel that their dreams will never come true and that God had forsaken them. The secret is to understand that God speaks life into situations. He doesn't speak and then mysteriously withdraw again. *God daily inspires His people by giving solutions to problems, ideas for creativity, and wisdom needed in business transactions. He speaks and He will certainly speak again.*

After receiving God's sound and proper impartation, we need to grasp every opportunity to speak with the same clarity and exactness. We are not to proclaim religious probabilities, but sound, heavenly doctrine.

1 Kings 17:2 Then the word of the Lord came to him.

Elijah received a word from God in a very challenging time and he obeyed promptly. In this season of his life, he was experiencing supernatural provision. Against all odds, scavenging ravens brought Elijah food. He survived the drought and then received another proceeding word from God to move on from that specific location. If Elijah had chosen to stay at the creek, it could have steered towards disaster. His decision to obey the word of the Lord has again transferred him into a new season of miracles where he had experienced the supernatural provision of oil. He even raised a widow's son from the dead in this remarkable season.

We may possess faith to move mountains but we may never move them if we religiously hold on to an 'out of season' word from God.

God doesn't change His mind, but He does operate in seasons. He regulates the seasons and He gives regular instructions. We have the option of moving with God, or staying behind. God may have revealed things to us many years ago, but He is currently giving us recurring substance regarding the previous instruction. The best thing we can do is to flow with the river of God's direction for our lives. Stubbornness, disobedience and offense are some of the things that may keep us out of the perfect will of God.

We should never allow our love and passion for God to dry up in the scorching heat of our own arrogance. We should repent and move on with God. We should catch up with Him every day and receive His heartbeat for our future. Like Elijah, we are on the brink of another miracle in our walk with God.

1 Chronicles 14: 10 And David inquired of God.

The Philistines constantly raided against King David and his people. David was prepared for warfare at any time and at any place, but he also understood the importance of receiving a word from God. He didn't want to make his own

THE WORD OF GOD|👑

plan. He desired to do the will of God. David was praying at this particular time and the Lord gave him permission to attack the enemy. God went before him and there was no chance of David losing the battle. He won an overwhelming victory against the Philistines.

When we seek the will of God in all circumstances, we will always be victorious. The battle scars will show on our lives, but the trophy will be in our hands. Although the Lord Jesus Christ has won the ultimate war between good and evil, we still need to fight many daily battles. We enter every battle as conquerors as we stand upon the word of the Lord. We believe and proclaim the victory according to the word of God; therefore the conquest belongs to us. As life goes on, the battles will continue and the victories will become purer. As anticipated, soon after this faith-experience, David was challenged into battle again.

1 Chronicles 14:14 Therefore David inquired again of God.

It is wonderful to read how this mighty king decided to inquire of the Lord for a second time. It was a very good option to take, as God did not give David approval to attack the enemy this time. The benefit of a proceeding word from the Lord is that we will align ourselves with His present plans and purposes for our lives. David did not just assume that he is sanctioned to attack the enemy again. He received a total different strategy from God the second time around. Without launching an attack on the enemy this time, he won an overwhelming victory again.

We have to consult with the Lord concerning daily strategies in regards to our children, finances, churches, and lives in general. By only 'going through the motions' in our lives, hidden passiveness is revealed. We may be doing the same 'good' thing for many years but we may still feel empty and displeased. Although these things may be good, it doesn't mean that God wants us to fall into the pitfalls of religious routines.

KINGDOM AUTHORITY

Without a proceeding word from God our holy habits, intimate intentions, and Sunday sacraments may lead to a dead end. We may be preparing serious sermons, praying for radical revival, fasting for spiritual solidarity, constructing beautiful buildings, composing sweet songs, or pioneering a national network of connections for all Christians of all churches; but all of this may be to no avail. Spiritual rivers may dry up. Spiritual battles may be lost. We may find ourselves going around the same mountain instead of pursuing God- ordained instructions for reaching our ultimate destination.

We need to be on the front foot, always one step ahead of the enemy and his tactics. A dear friend put it this way recently: "We shouldn't just know that there is an enemy in the bush, armoured with a bow and arrow. We should be alert enough to actually hear the squeak of the bow as the enemy prepares to release his fiery attack. Then we will be able to take the initiative away from the enemy, and surprise him with our own launching strategy."

We need to operate with the divine strategies of God. We have to receive regular instructions from heaven, bringing exactness to our walk with God on planet earth.

——————————

Psalms 119 reveals several approaches we might investigate in order to activate the authority of the word of God* in our own lives: (Numbers of verses are written in brackets)

* We can walk in it. The word of God is our light and our path. It gives us clear direction and protects us on our way. (1)
* We can keep it. The word of God is close to our hearts. It is a gift of intimacy, which enhances our personal relationship with God. Everyone needs this gift. (2)
* We can learn it. The word of God is the global curriculum for all knowledge and wisdom. It should be communicated in every school, college and university. (3)

74

* We can hide it in our hearts. The word of God is our spiritual treasure. It is hidden, but it will be revealed in heavenly moments. (4)

* We can meditate on it. The word of God is our constant emphasis. Daily meditation on the word will result in success and prosperity. (15)

* We can remember it. The word of God is our present and future inheritance. To forget the word will result in spiritual death and eternal emptiness. (16)

* We can live it. The word of God is our entire existence. It is our daily bread for substance, energy, and victory. (17)

* We can trust in it. The word of God is our heavenly super fund and offers us more than just financial security. It is not a resource for material possessions, but an everlasting heavenly security. (42)

* We can seek it. The word of God is our treasure. It is to be discovered day-to-day. Mysteriously, there are always more to find. Even when we read the same scripture several times, it might have multiple clarifications. (45)

* We can speak it. The word of God gives us expression. Speaking the word brings forth life. Dry bones in any valley will be awakened when it hears the distinguished sound of the word of God. (46)

* We can delight in it. The word of God is our joy. If we delight ourselves in the Lord and in His word, we will inevitably become delightful people; walking on straight paths with God. (47)

* We can sing about it. The word of God is our song. It brings the melody of heavenly songs into our worlds. It gives us a reason to smile, sing and dance. (54)

* We can believe it. The word of God is true and trustworthy. There is not a lot of truth in the world, but we can always rely on God's word. (66)

* We can hope in it. The word of God called us from our dark past. It will sustain us today and it will transfer us into a great future. (81)

* We can search it. The word of God is near. We can look for it, ask for it, and knock on heaven's door. We will find it. (82)
* We can consider it. The word of God is our only option in life. We should consider it over all other possibilities. (95)
* We can love it. The word of God is our life-long companion. We live with the word. We eat and drink the word. We can just fall in love with it. (97)
* We can follow it. The word of God leads us gently and clearly into our blessed future. There is always light at the end of the tunnel. (105)
* We can take it as a heritage. The word of God is our haven. It provides us with the promises of generational benefits. (111)
* We can perform it. The word of God gives us influence in this world. If we talk and walk the word, the world will never be the same. When we preach the word, the miracles will be the evidence. ('Heavenly performance' and not worldly entertainment) (112)
* We can observe it. The word of God is always visible. We need to perceive the word with faith, and not scientifically. Pre- conceived ideas will make our observations null and void. (117)
* We can know it. The word of God is a reality. We can be intimately acquainted with the word. There is no arrogance in memorizing scriptures. We can only be passionate about what we know. (125)
* We can long for it. The word of God essentially needs a partnership. We are the only books that people may ever read. Our yearning for the word will encourage the longing for salvation in the lives of unbelievers. (131)
* We should not turn from it. The word of God is a highway. It takes us places, and sometimes at high speeds. With the beautiful sight of the cross before us, we do not even contemplate turning to the left or to the right. (157)
* We should stand in awe of it. The word of God is awesome. It is mind-blowing, indescribable, and supernatural. (161)
* We can choose it. The word of God is like a real gentleman.

It invites, guides and instructs us gently. It always gives us a choice. (173)

———————————-

Revelations 19: 13 He was clothed with a robe dipped in blood, and His name is called 'the Word of God'.

The first chapter of the *Book of John* teaches us that Jesus is the Word of God and that He existed from the very beginning. Amazingly, He became a man and revealed God's grace and salvation to all mankind. He freely gave His life away; and even one of the robust soldiers at the scene of the cross confirmed that Jesus was the Son of God. He is the 'Word'.

Isaiah 40:8 The grass withers, the flower fades, but the word of our God stands forever.

Isaiah 55:10,11 For as the rain comes down, and the snow from heaven, and do not return there, but water the earth, and make it bring forth and bud, that it may give seed to the sower and bread to the eater, so shall My word be that goes forth from My mouth; It shall not return to Me void, but it shall accomplish what I please, and it shall prosper in the thing for which I sent it.

We are the words that God spoke before the foundation of the earth. God called us by our names and then He declared eternal promises of prosperity and blessings over us. His words were not just creative declarations over the earth and all the plants and animals. His words were explicitly proclaimed over the people He created in His image.

We should operate with fervent faith in the eternal purposes of God's promises concerning our future. We serve a God who is alive and well on planet earth. He loves to speak. He is releasing instructions right now to His faith-followers.

7

THE DWELLING PLACE

OF THE LORD

God created the entire universe. It is impossible just to imagine where He essentially lives. The Bible teaches us that heaven is God's throne and the earth is His footstool. But where is God's house?

In the Old Testament Solomon built God an amazing tabernacle. This became a holy place of worship. In New Testament times though, the focus has changed from law to grace, and from religious regulations to real relationship. As the Father of the biggest family ever, God is building himself an incredible mansion.

Hebrews 3:4 For every house is built by someone, but He who built all things is God.

Hebrews 3:5a & 6a And Moses indeed was faithful in all His house... But Christ as a Son over His own house, whose house we are.

Many scholars will be sad to realize that God's heart is actually not after a physical building, but a spiritual house. He desires personal relationships with real people. God is building a spiritual house and it will be indescribable in magnificence and splendor. He is building a dwelling place that does not consist of brick and mortar, but it consists of flesh and bones.

We are the house that God is building. God is not in a hurry as He is building a house of quality and perfection, even though to us it may seem that this project is taking forever and a day.

Our mindsets have to change from thinking about a futuristic mansion, to the realization that God has made His abode in us; the children of God. He builds, and then He restores bits and pieces. He continues to build as He imparts His character to His people on a daily basis. He already lives in us, but He never stops building; until the day of perfection.

The traditional opinions of scholars are that God is preparing a house in heaven for each one of us, but this is completely inaccurate. God is a family God, and He wants all of us to abide in one spiritual dwelling; right here and now. God is the creator of this house. Jesus Christ is the cornerstone of the house. The Holy Spirit brings God and man together in an immaculate building- and we all live happily, now and ever after.

Father God always intended to have genuine relationships. Not only are the Father, the Son, and the Holy Spirit in a perfect relationship, but God also desired a similar relationship with Adam. God started an amazing building project in the Garden of Eden, and called it Paradise. His relationship with Adam was one of perfect harmony and unison. God just wanted to live here. His heart was to walk and talk with Adam. But sadly this wonderful relationship was destroyed through sin and shame. The house was demolished.

THE DWELLING PLACE OF THE LORD|

When Jesus connected with mankind, the renovation started; a heavenly funded building project. God chose to construct His residence in mankind. The finished work of Jesus Christ would forever assure that sin and shame could not destroy this relationship again. The flesh of this house can become sick and old, and the bones of this house can be broken, but the house of God can never be destroyed again.

Ephesians 2:19-22 You are fellow citizens with the saints and members of the household of God,* having been built on the foundation of the apostles and the prophets, Jesus Christ# Himself being the chief cornerstone, in whom the whole building, being fitted together, grows into a holy temple in the Lord, in whom you also are being built together for a dwellingplace^ of God in the Spirit.

* But are fellow citizens with Christ's people. (TCNT)
* You belong to God's [own] household. (Amp)
* You are a building, which has been reared on the foundation of the Apostles and Prophets. (Wey)
# The actual foundation stone being Christ Jesus himself. (Phi)
# Through him every part of the building is closely united. (Gspd)
# In Him the whole structure is joined [bound, welded] together harmoniously. And it continues to rise [grow, increase]. (Amp)
^ To make a house wherein God may dwell. (Con)
^ For a habitation of God through the Spirit. (KJV)
^ To become a fixed abode for God through the Spirit. (Wey)
^ Into a spiritual dwelling for God. (NEB)

      The ultimate foundation of this incredible structure includes Jesus Christ (the cornerstone), as well as the apostles, and prophets; (the pillars). This great building is not made with building blocks, wood, or concrete, but with living stones. All the saints are the living units, and subsequently an amazing building is appearing in the earth. This building

KINGDOM AUTHORITY

is like a hidden gem, a treasure to be discovered.

The house of God is incredibly significant, and it is also described in the Bible as Mount Zion, the city of the living God *(Hebrews 12:22). This is not a city in heaven, but a heavenly city.* This is not a futuristic house that may possibly one day be occupied by good tenants in heaven. We are the living tenants that form and display the house of God as we live here on the earth today.

The saints of God who died in Christ are heavenly contributors to the building of the final stages of God's ultimate estate on the earth. They are now abiding in a wonderful and glorious dimension in the heavens. They are waiting for a reunion between heaven and earth. The saints are now encouraging God's people here on earth to strive towards immortality. They would love us to become the most incredible mansions of God on the earth.

1 Timothy 3:15 That you may know how you ought to conduct yourself in the house of God, which is the church of the living God, the pillar and the ground* of truth.

* The pillar and the foundation of the truth. (Gspd)
* And support of the truth. (Ber)
* And mainstay of the truth. (Mon)
* And base of what is true. (Bas)
* And foundation upon which the truth rests. (Knox)

We are the church of God on the earth today. We are God's family and co-workers. We are His extended hands. We are God's voice. God created a support program to reveal the reality of His truth in the earth. He decided to lay a foundation and build the church. The church is not supposed to be the world's laughing stock because of little defects in the structure. We are the most powerful spiritual force in this
82

earthly dimension.

Although people may experience a wonderful family

time in any church through praise, worship, preaching, praying, and fellowship, *the church is ultimately designed by God to be more than just a place of celebration or worship*. The church is God's earthly management structure. We were never established to be merely an organization, but to actually be a living organism in the earth.

As the house of God, the church is the ultimate governance, the supreme distributor of heavenly resources, and the only place of healing and salvation to all people. The church is everywhere; and at all times. We can play church once or twice a week, or we can impact the nations with the glory of God. We are the real dwelling place of God that brings salvation and healing to all the nations in the earth today.

1 Corinthians 3:16 Do you not know* that you are the temple of God and that the Spirit of God dwells^ in you?

* Do you not discern and understand that you [the whole church] are God's temple [His sanctuary], and that God's Spirit has His permanent dwelling in you [to be at home in you, collectively as a church and also individually]? (Amp)
^ *And that God's Spirit has his home in you.* (TCNT)

God is Spirit. He lives in us. We are His home, His dwelling place, and His abode. God is tangible. He is very close to us. This seems too good to be true, but it is true and it is real. God is constantly in the home, and He never changes address. We may walk away from home, but the Father abides eternally in His estate. He bought the house with the most expensive currency of all- the blood of His own Son, Jesus Christ.

We are the house of God. We are not for sale or for rent. We are occupied by the living God. He paid the mortgage and

83

there are no outstanding bills. He can now enjoy His eternal dwelling. Our lives have become living homes of the Most High God. Our Father lives in our hearts.

KINGDOM AUTHORITY

1 Peter 2:4,5 Coming to Him as to a living stone, rejected indeed by men, but chosen by God and precious, you also, as living stones, are being built up as a spiritual house, a holy priesthood, to offer up spiritual sacrifices acceptable to God through Jesus Christ.

Each one of us is a living brick in the spiritual house that God is building. One by one we bring beauty and glory to this amazing building. Collectively we bring a spiritual offering to our God, through our Lord Jesus Christ. This is an active offering and is given to God through the living of our lives. No animal or person would ever need to be slaughtered again to bring pleasure to our God. As living stones, our lives are the spiritual sacrifices that God desires. We are chosen stones, and the least we can do is to thank God by living lives that will bring honour to His name. As His holy priests we bring this sacrifice daily.

Our lives are a constant offering of praise and worship to God at home, in the work place, with our friends, and with the people we talk to every day. We can only succeed in this process by drawing very near to the precious living stone, Jesus Christ Himself. God chose Him, and God chose us. More than two thousand years ago Jesus Christ was totally rejected by men. Today we acknowledge and salute Him. We want to represent Him well in the earth. We want to reflect His perfect image to the world. When people look at us, they should see the most beautiful and perfect house that has ever been built.

————————————

John 14:2 In My Father's house are many mansions; if it were not so, I would have told you. I go to prepare a place for you.

This chapter confirms again that our God is a family God. The

context of this passage is the house of God, and not the 👑
heaven of God. Illuminating this is the fact that I counted
twenty-six   referrals to the word 'Father' in this whole chapter,
with

THE DWELLING PLACE OF THE LORD|

absolutely no referrals to 'heaven'.

Amazingly, we were taught for decades that the many mansions are in heaven, and not in the house of God. There is a clear difference between the Father's heaven and the Father's house.

When Jesus mentioned that He is going to prepare a place for His followers, He referred to the cross, and not heaven. He spoke these words just before His crucifixion. He was speaking about the house of the Father. He was referring to a place of security, safety, embrace, and love that can only be   obtained through intimacy with the Father. He was on His way to prepare that amazing spiritual place for all of us. This place in the house of the Father is not futuristic. It is available right here, right now. It has been available for millions of people over the past centuries, and many have already entered that place in the Father's house.

Finding our place in the house of God through Jesus Christ is most probably the closest position we can obtain to the heavenly dimension. Jesus is the way, the truth and the life. *(John 14:6)* This place is so real, so good, and so absolutely wonderful. It is eternal, which means we never have to 'long' for heaven. *(See Chapter 11).*

It is so easy to base our theories on possible futuristic events- things we hope will happen. God is currently building a heavenly house on earth, and not an earthly house in heaven. He needs kingdom builders and not church buildings.

God is looking for people who would advance His kingdom on the earth, and not just for people who want a ticket to heaven. Heaven is perfect and it is waiting for perfection on the earth. Jesus did not promise to prepare a place for us in heaven, as He wants us to be positioned on the earth for as long as possible. The longer we can stay on the earth, the more people might be transferred from the kingdom of darkness into the house of God. People who are

KINGDOM AUTHORITY

lost in sin and shame can find a shelter and a place of healing in the house of God. They will not find salvation on the promises of a heavenly hope, but on the reality of a heavenly home with hope and love right here on planet earth. There is still place in the house of God for billions of people and we trust the Lord that many nations will turn to Him.

Psalms 27:4 One thing I desired of the Lord, that I may dwell^ in the house of the Lord all the days of my life, to behold* the beauty of the Lord.

* To view the delightfulness. (Rhm)
* To enjoy the graciousness. (DeW)
* To enjoy the sweetness. (Jerus)
^ To dwell in the house of the Lord all the days of my life, that I may gaze on the loveliness of the Lord. (NAB)
^ That I may dwell in the house of the Lord [in His presence] all the days of my life, to behold and gaze upon the beauty [the sweet attractiveness and the delightful loveliness] of the Lord and to meditate, consider, and inquire in His temple. (Amp)

David displayed an amazing passion for the house of God. He just wanted to be close to God and experience the beauty and sweetness of this relationship. No wonder David wrote so many worship songs. He understood the grace of God, and he always desired to be in that dwelling place with the Father.

Psalms 92:13 Those who are planted in the house of the Lord shall flourish in the courts of our God.

God doesn't want His children to run away from His

house. We live and work in this world, but we live and work according to the rules of our Father. We are planted in His house. We have an eternal relationship with our Creator. He saved us and called us, and now He has established us in His house.

THE DWELLING PLACE OF THE LORD|

We are not forced to be in the house of God. We have a choice. But we shouldn't go astray like the prodigal son. It doesn't matter what the world has to offer. There is nothing that can compare with the love and security we experience in the Father's house. If we don't uproot ourselves from the house of the Lord, we will forever flourish with the prosperity and blessings of the Father.

8

LIVING IN THE MIRACULOUS

I was reading the local newspaper at a coffee shop recently when my eyes caught a column where somebody wrote the following: 'Sure, I believe in God. Now where are the miracles?' I was reminded once again that the world has heard enough of our promises. It wants to see the real thing behind the promises, the practical manifestation of what we say we represent.

Matthew 4:23-25 And Jesus went about all Galilee, teaching in their synagogues, preaching the gospel of the kingdom, and healing all kinds of disease among the people. Then His fame went throughout all Syria; and they brought to Him all sick people who were afflicted with various diseases and torments, and those who were demon-possessed, epileptics, and paralytics; and He healed them. Great multitudes followed Him.

Matthew 10:1,7 & 8 And when He had called His twelve disciples to Him, He gave them power over unclean spirits, to cast them out, and to heal all kinds of sickness and all kinds of disease. And as you go, preach, saying, 'The kingdom of God is at hand. Heal the sick, cleanse the lepers, raise the dead, and cast out demons. Freely you have received, freely give.'

We are supposed to proclaim the kingdom of God. We need to do this with boldness and courage, believing that our God will manifest His word and keep His promises. First of all we need to take action and actually do something. We need to put our money where our mouths are, to preach the kingdom and demonstrate the reality of the kingdom with powerful signs and wonders.

Mark 16:17,18 And these signs will follow those who believe: In My name they will cast out demons; they will speak with new tongues; they will take up serpents; and if they drink anything deadly, it will by no means hurt them; they will lay hands on the sick, and they will recover.

Jesus was a sought after preacher, and when He preached, signs and wonders followed Him. Jesus Christ is our perfect example of righteousness, peace, and living in the miraculous. He laid a solid foundation on the earth and started a revolution that will snowball until the end of days. His kingdom is ever increasing, ever progressing, and never-ending. The occurrence of signs, wonders, and miracles was not meant to be a distinct performance—*Jesus Christ has activated the miraculous on the earth, so that greater works can continue through His disciples. The days of miracles have only just begun.*

Jesus Christ's ministry established an excellent foundation for His disciples to continue the display of His supernatural power through the ages. In His time, Jesus had to travel from city to city to preach the Gospel of the kingdom and to perform miracles.

However, He was one man among many who needed a touch of the supernatural. Today, thousands of powerful men and women of God are doing exactly what Jesus taught them to do, and this domino effect will change the world forever. Jesus and His first twelve disciples transformed cities, and brought revival to a handful of nations over two thousand years ago. Jesus and thousands of His modern-day disciples will fill the whole earth with the glory of God. *This is not the time to debate, doubt, or criticize miracles, but to perform them, and to step into the glory that God has prepared for the earth.*

Acts 8: 4-19 shows us two different categories of supernatural power. On the one hand, we have Simon, the evil sorcerer of the city. On the other hand, Philip, the powerful, visiting evangelist:

Simon practiced sorcery in the city. He astonished all the people with his power over a long period of time and was recognized by the inhabitants of the city. Then Philip arrived in town and began preaching the kingdom of God. He performed signs and miracles; the paralyzed and lame walked again, people were healed and unclean spirits were cast out. Simon desired the power of the kingdom of God because he recognized the reality of the supernatural. He believed, was baptized and followed Philip. Simon was not satisfied with the counterfeit, for it could not bring fulfillment or satisfaction into his world. He knew that he needed the genuine, miraculous power of God. He believed, and hence he entered into an incomparable supernatural dimension.

1 Corinthians 4:20 For the kingdom of God is not in word but in power.

Heavens' supernatural dimension represents love, joy, and a selfless lifestyle of giving and sharing. Simon stepped into the freedom, acceptance, forgiveness and purpose that God had prepared for him.

KINGDOM AUTHORITY

Mat 24:14 And this gospel of the kingdom will be preached in all the world as a witness to all the nations, and then the end will come.

The Gospel is the good news of salvation and reconciliation in Jesus Christ. The spreading of the Gospel is our mandate on the earth, and Jesus only asks for our obedience and passion to fulfill this clear command. *The Gospel of the kingdom* is something completely different. It obviously *includes* the Gospel of salvation, but *adds* the dimension of supernatural living. The Gospel of the kingdom will activate people in all the nations of the earth to experience the fullness and the glory of God.

The church needs to bring people to maturity in Christ. *The news to be told is not just the good news of salvation, but it is the better news of the supreme and supernatural reign of Christ on the earth.* The end will not come before the church will realize our true assignment; preaching the power, supremacy, and the complete dominion of Christ and His people, on planet earth. Believing, implementing, and preaching this total future superiority, will bring finality and perfection to our earthly dimension, and all nations will recognize, acknowledge, and honor the King and His kingdom.

Mark 1:14,15 Jesus came to Galilee, preaching the gospel of the kingdom of God, and saying; 'The time is fulfilled,* and the kingdom of God is at hand. Repent, and believe in the gospel.

* The [appointed period of] time is fulfilled [completed]. (Amp)
* And the reign of God is near. (Gspd)
* The kingdom of God has arrived. (Phi)
* Time's up! God's kingdom is here. (Mes)

Jesus Christ is the supreme king and leader of the kingdom of God. He is a relational leader, and not a religious fanatic. A kingdom mindset opposes the disillusionment that religiosity
92

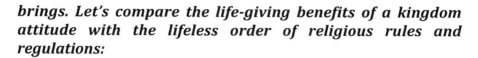
brings. Let's compare the life-giving benefits of a kingdom attitude with the lifeless order of religious rules and regulations:

- A kingdom mindset will activate the heavenly forces of power and authority in us. Religiosity consists of talking and debating; an endless cycle of natural, empty activities.
- A kingdom mindset will release healings and miracles in our lives. Religiosity will explain the miraculous away; reasoning that the days for the supernatural are long gone, and that we should just be content with the way things are.
- A kingdom mindset includes a supernatural lifestyle, expecting miracles daily and regularly. Religiosity focuses only on knowledge and performance; going through the conscience-driven motions rather than a Spirit-led lifestyle.
- A kingdom mindset proclaims that 'Jesus Christ is *Lord*'. It entails choosing Him as our Savior as well as honoring His supreme authority. It allows partnership. Religiosity will allow us to accept Jesus as our *Savior* only. It won't allow too much personal growth in God. It just allows spiritual slavery.
- A kingdom mindset is Biblically based on the three pillars of righteousness, peace and joy; which are the solid   ingredients of a great relationship. *(Rom 14:17)* Religiosity brings condemnation, strife and stirs up rebellion in peoples' lives. The potential liberty of a relationship with a savior turns into the fear of judgment of a God who is a consuming fire.
- A kingdom mindset announces an ever-increasing hope towards the most amazing future for God's people on the earth. It envisions the amazing reign of Christ and His kingdom on the earth. Religiosity always reveals doom and gloom' interpretations of the future of

the church. These ideas point to a hopeless situation for God's people under the reign of a super-human antichrist.

Mat 6:33 But seek first the kingdom of God* and all his righteousness, and all these things shall be added to you.

* But continue to seek first. (Mon)
* Set your heart on his kingdom. (Phi)
* Pursue the Kingdom and God's goodness first. (Rieu)
* First be eager to have God as your King. (Beck)
* But you must make his kingdom your greatest care. (Gspd)
* But seek [aim at and strive after] first of all His kingdom [His way of doing]. (Amp)
* Give your entire attention to what God is doing right now. (Mes)

This amazing scripture is all about priorities. It is about faith and not about religious rituals. It doesn't say: 'Seek only', but 'seek first'. The kingdom of God will be insignificant if we reduce it to function exclusively in terms of spiritual priorities. If we only pray, preach, read the Bible, and thereby separate ourselves from the real world, we will become spiritual spectators with no influence. To pursue the kingdom of God is to strive to do His will every day. He wants us to grasp the kingdom, believe it, live in it, and have this as our first priority.

Material things, family, religious activities, blessings, prosperity, business ventures, sport, vision, health, education, housing, clothing and even church life, should be secondary priorities in our lives. It is not about my possessions, my ministry, my gift, or my needs anymore. It is about His daily reign in my life. If we can prioritize correctly, we will experience the sovereign provision of God every day, in every area of our lives.

––––––––––––––––

I remember going to my dentist in Durban, South Africa, in the late nineties. She was a wonderful Christian lady and we had many conversations about God over a number of years. On one particular day, she was preparing to begin a procedure and asked me to open my mouth. She paused, and exclaimed with excitement: 'I see you have received a blessing'. I didn't understand, and couldn't ask her to explain what she meant because of all the instruments in my mouth. I had to ask her a while later about her comment. *She told me there was a perfect layer of gold in one of my regular fillings.* The dentist understood that this must have been supernatural, as she had never given me a gold filling, and my dental records confirmed this fact.

This miracle occurred without me even knowing it had happened. I didn't have specific tooth problems, and nobody prayed for me to receive a gold filling. I knew other people all over the world had received similar supernatural healings and blessings and, to my astonishment, I was one of those. I was overwhelmed and treasure this experience as a miraculous intervention from the living God. I still have the gold filling, and I am now using this experience to witness to my current dentist.

Perhaps it happened because I needed a miracle at a very challenging phase of my life- a gentle whisper from the Holy Spirit to confirm the great love that God has for me- I don't know- all I know is that the filling is still in my mouth today, a perfect layer of gold. It is a miracle. Every now and again my wife, Millanie, asks me to open my mouth, just to have a quick glimpse of the miracle of gold. I have never been a follower of miracles in particular, but I love and desire the supernatural. As I have chosen to follow Jesus, I believe miracles will follow me.

This is what living in the miraculous is all about from a kingdom perspective. If we are in any way still carnally minded, we would struggle to understand the miraculous. Our fleshly, stubborn hearts have to be replaced with gentle, receptive ones in order to grasp the supernatural. Living in the miraculous is a lifestyle. We don't all need to receive a gold filling, have a cancer healed or a headache vanish supernaturally to experience the miraculous. Getting parking close to the entrance of the busiest mall in the city, or even receiving a specific amount of money at the perfect time of need is living supernaturally. It can include your children receiving an opportunity to travel overseas as well as the healing that took place when you prayed for a sick person. Living in the miraculous means enjoying an exciting life; a life with more positives than negatives, because we can allow our supernatural God to display himself in our lives in a supernatural way.

Our own distorted, religious ideas and man-made doctrines can prevent us from living in the miraculous. Our own ideologies, philosophies, limited mindsets, and lack of vision need to be transformed into a passion and desire to see the greater works of Christ. Jesus himself desires that we step into the supernatural dimension.

John 14:12 Most assuredly, I say to you, he who believes in Me, the works that I do he will do also; and greater works than these he will do, * because I go to My Father.

* And he will do even greater things than these. (Phi)

Everything we have ever believed, even well cemented doctrines, has to be laid at the Potter's feet for reconstruction. If we are unwilling to be totally transformed into new creations in Christ, we will find ourselves permanently trying to scale obstacles that obscure the potential of us living in the miraculous.

Some use prayer, fasting, consecration, sacrifices, a solitary lifestyle, poverty, and even physical pain to obtain mystical and supernatural powers, but the Biblical way to step into the supernatural realm is by faith in the living God.

Elijah's faith in God shocked hundreds of prophets of Baal as they were trying their best to invoke a demonstration of power from a dead god. They even performed rituals to a degree of self-destruction.

Elijah found this funny and even mocked them, asking if their god could be on a holiday. Elijah's faith in God initiated an incredible fireworks display. The supernatural was activated by his prayer of faith and demonstrated in the physical realm by heaven's fire *(1 Kings 18)* I wish I could see that!

Today, we need to imitate Elijah's trust in God. We need a kingdom mentality. It is not about us anymore, but about God in us, before us, and around us. We don't have to perform rituals, and we don't have to harm ourselves. All we need to do to experience God's fire from heaven is to believe and trust that God will actually perform it.

9

KINGDOM PRAYER

I am a morning person. I wake early, wash my face, grab a cup of coffee, and sit at the table to pray and read my Bible. I don't view this like an obligation, but rather like an opportunity to be blessed. I don't think we should ever pray in response to a sense of obedience to any law. We should make it easy, and make it enjoyable. Pray while you work or play, pray before or after lunch, pray in the morning or at night, pray in your car or in the shower. Just pray.

Prayer should be a lifestyle, not merely an act of adherence to a law. Prayer is relational; by it we connect with God heart- to-heart.

Luke 6:12 Now it came to those days that He went out to the mountain to pray, and continued all night in prayer to God.

Jesus understood the importance of connecting with His Father through prayer. He never initiated an action before speaking to His Father. Jesus' ministry success on earth was, in part, the result of Him praying regularly. We see this explained when Jesus said: 'I do only what I see my Father doing'. Jesus' prayerful lifestyle led to His capacity to carry His Father's heart, and to know what His Father would do in any given situation. His wonderful ministry of salvation, healing and power was built on a lifestyle of prayer.

For Jesus, spending time with the Father was like breathing, like having regular meals. He needed these inspirational times of solitary intimacy with His Father. He manifested natural signs and wonders after connecting with His spiritual source.

Mark 1:38 Now in the morning, having risen a long while before daylight, He went out and departed to a solitary place and there He prayed.

If Jesus would identify the importance of prayer in every day life, we should unquestionably follow His example. He was the sinless Son of God, but has displayed His total dependence on His Father through prayer. He never did His own thing!

John 5:19 Most assuredly, I say to you, the Son can do nothing of Himself, but what He sees the Father do; for whatever He does, the Son also do in like manner.

Jesus always obeyed the voice of His Father. In the kingdom of God, we should pursue total obedience to the Father. We should not be listening to any other voices. The plans and purposes of God for His people are revealed in our lives through the voice of the Father deep inside our own hearts. It is like having heaven in your heart. We don't have to perform to embrace an open heaven. Heaven is open, and God speaks clearly, and regularly.

In *Matthew 6:5 Jesus said: 'And when you pray'.* He didn't say: 'If you pray.' Prayer is a pleasure, not a duty. Prayer is an outworking of our love for God. As people speak to their friends, we should speak to our best Friend. God desires to hear our voices as we reach out to Him. More essentially, He would love for us to hear His voice.

Sometimes we whisper, sometimes we cry out—it doesn't really matter, as long as we connect with our Creator, and quiet our hearts to hear His instructions. Our prayers should be natural as breathing; not complicated by rules and regulations about what to say or how to say it. It should never become a task or a burden. Prayer is the result of a relationship between a Father and a child. We connect with God to hear His heartbeat, and to experience His amazing love for us personally. As we draw close to Him, He will also draw near to us. *(James 4:8)*

Matthew 6:5,6 And when you pray, you shall not be like the hypocrites. For they love to pray standing in the synagogues and on the corner of the streets, that they may be seen by men.

But you, when you pray, go into your room, and when you have shut the door, pray to your Father who is in the secret place; and your Father who sees in secret will reward you openly.

Reading the New Testament, we find that some of the religious people of the day attempted to publicly impress others with their long, publicly recited prayers. Praying is not about sounding the trumpet of our own egos—God loves us, and wants us to meet Him in moments of solitude; moments in a car, in the street, at the supermarket, or at the beach; in fact absolutely anywhere! We can cultivate a daily spiritual practice that will lead us to a secret place of consistent intimacy with God. Here, we will experience moments of direction, wisdom, and reassurance from our Father.

Matthew 6:7 And when you pray, do not use vain repetitions as the heathen do. For they think they will be heard for their many words.

Repetitions are just words, nothing more than heathen mantras, and a complete waste of time. Prayer is not merely telling stories, hinting and playing the guessing game.

101

God knows what we need, and even what we want— we don't pray to inform Him of our requirements. Praying is an act of faith, because asking is believing that you will receive the things you ask for. Praying is making faith declarations according to God's wonderful promises in the Bible, trusting that it will come to pass. Praying is proclaiming His word.

These prayers are music in the ears of our Creator. We need to discern the difference between reminding God of His wonderful promises on the one hand, and the hollow repetition of religious and spiritual slogans on the other. Faith and kingdom power arise from the first, but pride and arrogance follow in the latter.

A long and wordy prayer is not necessarily an effective prayer.

Vain repetitions are ungodly and religious, and do not belong in the prayer vocabulary of God's kingdom people. We always pray from a position of victory. We pray with faith, even during difficult times.

We all would love to experience answered prayers on a regular basis. We can pray for hours, days, and months without having these breakthroughs. Jesus revealed the secret of *forgiveness.*

Matthew 6:14 For if you forgive men their trespasses, your heavenly Father will also forgive you.

Unforgiveness will cripple us spiritually. It will totally paralyze our being. By choosing not to forgive, we invite demonic influences into our world. We allow anger, criticism, anxiety, fear, hate, negativity, depression, sickness and even death to operate against us. Living with unforgiveness is dancing with the devil. The only way to experience total victory is to forgive and keep on forgiving.

Forgive yourself, forgive your enemies, and God will set you free. When we fail to forgive, we put ourselves in prison. (Matthew 18:23-35).

My natural father left my mother for another woman when I was about twelve years of age. This event had a huge impact on my life. This broken relationship with my natural father developed into a broken relationship with my heavenly Father. It actually had a negative impact on all the relationships I had at the time. For more than five years I neither visited nor contacted my dad. He visited me a few times at boarding school, where we barely managed a simple conversation. I was angry for what he had done, and did not even entertain the thought of forgiveness.

However, things changed completely after I gave my heart to the Lord, because the Lord changed me. I remember calling my dad one Sunday afternoon after church to tell him that I loved him, and that I forgave him for everything he had done. He burst into tears on the other side of the line, and could not speak at all. I don't recall him ever asking for forgiveness, but he never had to. Forgiveness is something we choose to do, whether it is asked for or not.

I forgave him, and I was free. Forgiveness brought restoration to our relationship and after all those years of hate and disconnection, I knew that something good could come out of all the pain. My dad was not set free yet, but I was totally free. He couldn't understand what had happened to me, but it spoke volumes to him that I was able to love him again. A seed was sown, and in God's perfect time, my dad gave his life to Christ as well!

———————————————-

Matthew 6:9-13 Our Father in heaven, hallowed be Your name. Your kingdom come, Your will be done on earth as it is in heaven. Give us this day our daily bread. And forgive us our debts, as we forgive our debtors. And do not lead us into temptation, but deliver us from the evil one. For Yours is the kingdom and the power and the glory forever. Amen.

God wants us to pray simple but passionate prayers of faith, believing and expecting results from the heavenly dimension. Jesus gave us this amazing prayer example as a heritage for all generations. It is not supposed to be religious rhetoric. It is not supposed to be five steps or seven keys to effective prayer- it is a practical example, a godly reality, and a powerful pattern for communicating with the Father. Jesus doesn't want us to become preoccupied with powerless poems, people- pleasing prayers, and professional proclamations.

This prayer is regularly used in international Christian circles, but Jesus never intended it to become religious poetry, or a popular public recital. He is interested in you and me— in our lives, our dreams, our challenges, our purpose, and our future. This prayer is designed to set you up for greatness in God. It is a solid foundation and a picture of kingdom reality.

Let us examine the phrases Jesus prayed through a topic, a verse, a short explanation, as well as a simple prayer example for each:

1. PRESENCE

* Matthew 6:9: Our Father in heaven, Hallowed be Your name.

Jesus desires that we will worship and honor our Heavenly Father. The prayer starts with adoration, reverence and respect. Addressing God as 'Our Father', and not as 'Almighty Creator', represents intimacy at the highest level. This is a prayer phrase of exaltation. We glorify our heavenly Father. It is personal. It is emotional. It is real. We can enter into our Father's presence through worship.

Prayer example:

'Our Father in heaven, I come to you today to intimately worship you. I want to be in your presence. You are my deliverer, my provider, my fortress and my comfort. You are my healer, my joy, and my strength. Father, you will never leave or forsake me. Thank you for your amazing love for me.'

***

2. DOMINION

* Matthew 6:10a Your kingdom come. Your will be done.

Jesus desires to establish His kingdom and His heavenly purpose on earth through His disciples. In this prayer portion we acknowledge His supreme authority as the Son of God. We also acknowledge His powerful reign as the King of heaven and earth. We seek His will and purpose for our lives, recognizing His perfect dominion over all things.

Prayer example:

'Father, I acknowledge your rule over my life. You are my Lord, the One with maximum authority. I pray that your kingdom come and that your will be done in my life today. I lay down my own selfish desires and personal ambitions. Lord, you are the King of kings, and the Lord of lords. Reign in me. Have dominion on the earth through me.'

***

3. RADIANCE

* Matthew 6:10b On earth as it is in heaven.

Jesus desires us to be both heavenly minded and earthly good. This is a good time to thank God for our connection with heaven. We can praise him for the access we have to heaven's riches, knowing that we can use heaven's power to our advantage every day. There is so much pain and sickness on the earth. We should pray that the Lord would release His heavenly radiance to our earthly dimension.

In our prayers, we should remember that heaven does not represent a futuristic adventure (Sweet bye and bye), but a current reality. We are seated in heavenly places in Christ Jesus. *(Ephesians 2:6b)* Heaven is the factory outlet of all the power, love, grace, goodness, glory, and perfect radiance of God pertaining to our daily lives- right here and now on planet earth.

Prayer example:

'Father, I thank you for the reality of heaven with all its perfection and beauty. Open the floodgates of heaven into my world today. Help me to stay connected with perfection, and to receive all the blessings, healing, and power that are available for me in this dimension. Lord, I pray that people would be able to draw life and prosperity from me today; and I ask to be earthly good.'

***

4. PROVISION

* Matthew 6: 11 Give us this day our daily bread.

Jesus wants us to pray for sunshine, rain, seed, soil, time and minerals. He wants us to pray for the ingredients, as well as a successful process of 'mixing and baking'. He never planned for us to take things for granted, or to have a survival mentality. Asking for daily bread implies praying, as well as working towards the process of perfect provision. Prayer is not just about food, but also about graffiti-free streets, crime-free suburbs, pollution-free cities, and war-free nations.

Prayer example:

'Father, I thank you for your supernatural provision in my world. I thank you for food, friends and fun in my life. I pray for my family, church, leaders, city council, as well as the leaders of our wonderful country. I ask that you will provide in all their needs, Lord. I pray for my neighbors, as well as for the people in our suburb, city, and nation.'

***

5. RESTORATION

* Matthew 6:12 And forgive us our debts, as we forgive our debtors.

Jesus desires that we will ask forgiveness, that we will forgive, and that we accept the fact that we are forgiven. Sin and shame will attempt to cling on us like dirt. Forgiveness cleanses us from all our hurt and shame. It erases the dirt and darkness forever. God's forgiveness is very expensive and brought compensation to mankind through the currency of blood. Jesus' atonement was sacrificial and permanent. His blood cleansed us completely and made us white as snow. We received perfect forgiveness, and now we can bring perfect restoration to this broken world.

Prayer example:

'Father, I accept your amazing and unconditional forgiveness in my life today. I refuse to look back to the sin and shame in my past. The blood of Jesus accomplished this perfect restoration, and I am so thankful. I choose to forgive every person who said or has done anything against me. Help me Lord, to never be offended and to always be a forgiving person.'

***

6. AUTHORITY

* Matthew 6:13a And do not lead us into temptation, but deliver us from the evil one.

      Jesus wants us to live in His accomplished victory. We are called to manifest His victory on the cross every day. God will not lead us into trouble, but He will test our faith through tribulations and difficult challenges. We never have to fall into a cycle of temptation, sin and deliverance. We can live in the overcoming power of the Holy Spirit. We can do all things through Jesus Christ, our Lord. When temptation assails us, we will declare the victory, and implement the power of the finished work of Christ. We have perfect authority over all the power of the enemy, and nothing shall by any means hurt us. *(Luke 10:19)*

Prayer example:

'Father, I thank You for the victory of the cross. Help me today to walk in the power of the finished work of my Lord Jesus Christ. Even when I face temptation today, I will not fall. I have authority over the evil one, in Jesus name.'

***

7. GLORY

* Matthew 6:13b For yours is the kingdom and the power and the glory forever. Amen.

      Jesus desires that we will represent Him accurately in the Father's kingdom. We are royal ambassadors of the Most High God. We exist to glorify God, and to bring high praises unto Him in the earth. Our prayers should reflect our stature in Christ. We are not the devil's puppets, but the worship vessels of our God. We should proclaim that the kingdom, power and glory belong to God, and to Him alone.

Prayer example:

This last portion of prayer can involve praise and worship. Play a CD, sing a song, and declare the glory of God into the atmosphere: *'Father, I declare your praises. I worship you alone. All power, authority, blessing, dominion, honor, and glory, belong to you. Lord, you are the Creator of heaven and earth. You reign supreme. I thank you for eternal life and daily strength to love and serve you. Amen.'*

***

Well, this is Jesus-style praying. This is throne-room praying, heavenly praying, and effective praying. Using this powerful pattern, will lead to real results in our prayer lives. We don't need to use the best vocabulary to receive the best results. We only need faith. We can only pray prayers of faith if we pray the word of God (in our own vocabulary). We can also read scriptures and then pray the promises of the word back to God. We need to be set free from any religious and church obligations in terms of how well and how long we pray. These legalistic requirements take the wind out of the sail of ordinary Christians.

Our prayers will get answered if they are loaded with positive, kingdom ingredients like:

- God focus.
- Kingdom mindset.
- Victorious attitude.
- Freedom from religious procedures and obligations.
- Fresh anointing of the Holy Spirit.
- Faith.
- Word-based declarations.
- Humility and love.
- Reverence.

KINGDOM AUTHORITY

- Heavenly connection.
- Holy Spirit impartation.
- Patience.

In contrast to the above, our prayers may not get answered when loaded with negative, anti-kingdom ingredients like:

- Conscience comforting content.
- Inaccurate philosophies.
- False statements.
- Self-motivated ambitions, ideas and aspirations.
- A pharisaical mindset.
- Total passivity.
- Incompetence.

———————————

James 5:15 And the prayer of faith will save the sick, and the Lord will raise him up. And if he has committed sins, he will be forgiven.

Our prayers should be faith driven, and the results will be miraculous. Faith prayers will channel health and prosperity into our worlds. We will rise in all areas of our lives. Our marriages will be marvelous. Our jobs will be joyful. Our finances will be fantastic. Our streets will be silent. Our kids will be kind. Not everything will be perfect, but everything will be a lot better. Many sick people would receive healing and the kingdom of God would advance even further.

James 5:16 Confess* your sins to one another, and pray for one another, that you may be healed. The effective, fervent prayer# of a righteous man avails much.

* Confess to one another your faults (your slips, your false steps, your offenses, your sins) and pray (also) for one another, that you may be healed and restored (to a spiritual tone of mind and heart). The earnest (heartfelt, continued)

prayer of a righteous man makes tremendous power available (dynamic in its working). (Amp)
Tremendous power is made available through a good man's earnest prayer. (Phi)
Powerful is the heartfelt supplication of a righteous man. (Wey)

God answers prayers. We can be effective prayer warriors. We need the dynamic influence of heartfelt prayers daily. Our passionate prayers will have powerful results. We need to constantly walk in humility and forgiveness with one another. It is basically impossible to be aggravated with your kingdom family and still have tremendous power. We should go back to the basic Bible principles, and the results will follow automatically.

———————————

1 Thessalonians 5:16,17 Rejoice always, pray without* ceasing.

* Pray constantly. RSV
* Never give up praying. Gspd

Prayer is not performance orientated, but relationship focused. It is about normal conversations with God, and about enjoying continuous quality time with Him. These conversations will include praise and worship, asking for help, thanksgiving, and even questioning. Prayer may require time, but it should become effortless as we realize the privilege that is ours.

Jude 1:20 But you, beloved, building yourselves up on your most holy faith, praying* in the Holy Spirit.

* Continue to pray in the power of the Holy Spirit. (Amp)

God understands all languages, but His first language is the language of the Holy Spirit. It is extremely beneficial for

111

our Christian walk, to accept and receive this wonderful language. It cannot be learned with human knowledge. The language of the Holy Spirit is a release from the river of heaven. This language is not just for a chosen few pastors, bishops, and priests. It is an added bonus that comes with the gift of salvation through Jesus Christ. We receive it by faith. We speak it by faith. We communicate mysteries with God. When you receive this amazing language, streams of living water will start flowing out of your innermost being. *(John 7:38)*

1 Corinthians 14:14,15 For if I pray in a tongue, my spirit prays, but my understanding is unfruitful. What is the conclusion then? I will pray with the spirit, and I will pray with the understanding.

By speaking in tongues we speak directly to God. We speak, sing and pray in a spiritual language. If we stop speaking in tongues, we will lose the benefit of Pentecost. We will lose the wind and the fire. We will lose the passion and the power. Our churches need this passion. The tongues are not the power, but it will bring the power. Speaking in tongues releases the passion that sometimes sits dormant inside of us. (And our churches). We need to flow with the river, or we will dry up. We need to have Holy Spirit-driven prayers, praise, and worship in our churches. We need to continue to do this. By speaking in tongues in our services, we may offend a few people, but we may also release fire from heaven that can bring thousands to Christ.

Revelation 5:8 Now when He had taken the scroll, the four living creatures and the twenty four elders fell down before the Lamb, each having a harp, and golden bowls full of incense, which are the prayers of the saints.

Revelation 8:3-5 Then another angel, having a golden censer, came and stood at the altar. He was given much incense that he should offer it with the prayers of the saints upon the golden altar, which was before the throne. And the smoke of the incense, with the prayers of the saints, ascended before God from the angel's hand. Then the angel took the censer, filled it with fire from the altar, and threw it to the earth. And there were noises, thunderings, lightning, and an earthquake.

Our God receives our prayers on a daily basis. It ascends to His throne, and are received in the heavenly dimension as a burned offering. When we pray, God's angels are activated to receive our prayers into a golden, heavenly vessel. The angels present this bowl as an offering unto God on a golden altar, before His golden throne.

Our requests, decrees, and supplications are transferred from our broken, earthly dimension to the perfect, supernatural, heavenly domain.

This amazing picture is not farfetched, unrealistic, or an animated fairy tale. In fact, this heavenly illustration gives us meaning for the moment, hope for the future, and passion to pursue our kingdom prayers on earth. This heavenly depiction shows us that time and space, or even demonic principalities, cannot restrict and intimidate the prayers we offer to God. On the contrary, our prayers penetrate the atmosphere like satellite wavelengths at the speed of light as our voices call out to God with fervent prayers of faith.

The angels receive, sort and prepare these passionate proclamations for further circulation. Religious, self-focused prayers most probably won't make it to heaven's satellite station. The faith-filled prayers, received by the angels, are then transferred into the golden super bowl, where it is treated, mixed, and released to God's throne. The heavenly ingredients that the angels add to the bowl bring perfect fragrance to the golden bowl. *And God answers our prayers.*

10

THE GOSPEL OF THE KINGDOM

Having read quite a number of books about the so called 'end times', I have always been astonished about how these writers could be so smart. These books were filled with structures, events, dates of events, timetables, historical data, possible wars, names of evil kings as well as predictions about the appearance of antichrists. They would pronounce the contradictory statements such as God's wrath over some countries on one hand, and His love for other countries on the other. Some speculated about worldwide terror, whilst others predicted the termination of the world.

All these theories and speculations have drawn my attention. Like so many Christians, I started to build my own doctrinal foundation based on the fairy tales in these books. I was so impressed by all the biblical references that I never checked if it was used in context. I wasn't alert to the fact that most of these books were sold in the 'novel' section of the Christian bookshops.

Sadly for these intellectuals, 'Armageddon' has never occurred when it was supposed to happen; and Jesus did not return when He should have returned. Subsequently, realizing that their integrity is at stake, these writers attempted to redeem themselves by writing new books with new dates, statistics and forecasts about future 'doom and gloom' events in the world.

The time for Christians to believe in fairy tales is over. Fables about beasts and dragons fighting an evil battle and destroying the people of God cannot be   believed anymore. These man-made theories show the ignorance of many preachers and writers. Everything that is noted in the Bible has to be assessed from the perspective of a victorious church. The 'end times' are explicitly about Jesus Christ and His manifested glory. People anticipate bad things to happen, but many of those things have already transpired.

There is just no way any person can make chronological predictions about the future of the earth, or the coming of the Lord Jesus Christ. We do not ignore the reality of demonic forces and evil principalities, but we are supposed to focus our attention on Jesus Christ, the author and finisher of our faith. *(Hebrews 12: 2)*. When we have a distorted picture of the end, we will never become a forceful kingdom who will influence the nations for Christ. The time has come for us to renounce fables, ideologies, and the doctrines of demons. *(1 Tim 4:1)* It is now the time to believe the word of the Lord without compromise.

———————————————-

Matthew 24:14 And the gospel of the kingdom will be preached in all the world as a witness to all the nations, and then the end will come.

The good news of the gospel is salvation through Jesus Christ. The gospel of the kingdom incorporates this remarkable salvation, but it also includes the dominion and the supreme authority of Jesus Christ over our lives.

Jesus Christ becomes our Savior when we hear the gospel of salvation, but He becomes our supreme Lord when we believe the preaching of the gospel of the kingdom.

Most nations on the earth have somehow been exposed to some form of gospel preaching through pulpit ministry, missionary outreaches, evangelistic campaigns, or personal testimonies from friends and family members. We now need to preach the gospel of the kingdom to all nations. The kingdom gospel^ will challenge nations not just to accept Jesus as their blessed Redeemer, *but also to submit completely under Christ's absolute rule and reign.* It basically implies the following:

^ Jesus is not just our King and Savior, but He is our Lord with maximum authority over our lives.

^ Our eternal future is not focused on a mansion in heaven, but on a victorious position of authority with Christ here on earth.

^ We are not slaves of sin or shame as we represent the Lord Jesus Christ with complete freedom.

^ Our Christian lives do not exist of religious obligations, but of victorious living. Instead of being busy with programs and religious duties, we focus on Holy Spirit power, healings, and miracles.

^ We are not part of an organization where we *have* to attend church meetings. We are part of a living organism called the body of Christ. We are the church- in a fulltime capacity.

^ We believe in sound, word-based doctrine, and not in man-made philosophies and ideas.

^ We believe that we will live supernatural and abundant lives; and not ordinary, conditional lives.

^ Instead of experiencing a lot of condemnation, strife, and struggle in our Christian walk, we experience the kingdom reality of righteousness, peace, and joy in the Holy Spirit. *(Romans 14:17)*

^ We are not just believers, but we are kings in the mighty kingdom of the King.
^ We do not only believe, but we have dominion to rule on the earth.

It is simple and practical. Jesus was never complicated, theoretical, or religious. Jesus proclaimed a simple gospel message but simultaneously announced that the kingdom of God was at hand. He also mentioned that the kingdom of God is within us *(Luke 17:21)*, and that within us rests the power of the Holy Spirit to change the world *(Acts 1:8)*. This power is dormant if we only know about it. The moment we activate this power and release it, we would be able to transform this world from its current state into the amazing plans and purposes that God has for His creation.

The nations need to experience the supreme power of the kingdom of God. Every tongue needs to confess that Jesus Christ is Lord. The radiance of the glory of God should become more eminent in our lifetimes than in any other century. Signs, miracles, and wonders should accompany our preaching in all churches, and in all nations.

On the other hand, we need to remember that evil and unrighteousness will progress simultaneously with the increasing of God's kingdom. *But good will conquer evil, and the kingdom of light will reign supreme in the end.*

The tabernacle of old consisted of three dimensions, which represents three levels of living: *Exodus 26:33,34; Exodus 40:8- 34.*

1. Outer court:

This dimension reflects a worldly lifestyle. It speaks of a life without God.

'I am living on the outside; in the courtyard. I need to enter into His presence to experience God's amazing reality in my

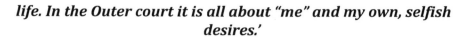

life. In the Outer court it is all about "me" and my own, selfish desires.'

    2. Holy place:

This dimension reflects the church of Jesus Christ on the earth.

'I acknowledge the reality of God but my life is still influenced by my own ambitions, as well as worldly desires. God is there for me when I need Him. In the Holy place it is all about "me" and God.'

    3. Most holy place:

This dimension reflects the beauty and perfection of heaven.

'Jesus is the center and the core of my total existence. I am not just saved and ready to go to heaven, but I declare the supreme rule of Christ in my life. In the Most holy place it is all about God!'

The ultimate presence of God can only be experienced in the 'Most holy place'. Living self- centered lifestyles (by giving God only a part-time role to play in our lives), will withhold us from experiencing the fullness that the kingdom holds. We will not arrive at the 'end' if we only preach the gospel of salvation. We need to preach the kingdom gospel, and then the end (completion, perfection) will come.

—————————————

I will outline a picture of life on the earth in the days of Noah. Grasping this reality may actually enhance our understanding about the comparison that Jesus made between His own return, and the days of Noah in the Old Testament. Many scholars through the ages have transformed this simple comparison into complex and complicated theories.

Matthew 24:37-39 But as the days of Noah were, so also will the coming of the Son of Man be, for as in the days before the flood, they were eating and drinking, marrying and giving in marriage, until the day that Noah entered the ark, and did not know until the flood came and took them all away, so also will the coming of the Son of Man be.

In the days of Noah people lived as if there were no tomorrow. They enjoyed life from day to day, and made no effort to please God. Sin prevailed to such a degree that God made the decision to terminate all the people on the earth. His intention was to destroy sin, and to give mankind a brand new beginning. But no one cared about God or His ways. Everyone was living for himself. The people worked, got married, enjoyed parties, and pursued their own cravings and desires. God was looking for a righteous man who would trust Him unconditionally; a man who would obey Him completely. God found Noah.

Noah and his family displayed integrity and righteousness before God. God chose Noah to pursue an incredible mission. This task was forever to be one of the strangest and most challenging projects given to any person. God required from Noah to build a ship on dry ground; a boat in a land that has never received rain in any shape or form. Noah and his family became the laughing stock of all the people.

Noah though, was willing to pursue the word of God in the face of immense persecution and criticism. Noah and his family were most probably threatened at times, as well as being exposed to violent behavior in public. Social groups probably targeted them, trying to stop this ridiculous pursuit of Noah and his family.

Many scholars misinterpreted Jesus' teachings in *Matthew 24*. Jesus taught a simple reality about the end of times, and used the story of Noah to make it easy to understand. He clearly stated that the coming of the Son of

Man would be like in the days of Noah. There are many similarities about the lifestyles of the people who lived in the days of Noah and the people who are currently dwelling on the face of the earth.^

^ The eight people on the boat represent the church of Jesus Christ. We are the righteous people chosen by God to remain on the earth. We will stand for God like Noah in the midst of trials and tribulations. Noah didn't plan to go anywhere but his strategy was to remain on the earth and to complete his assignment. Therefore we should plan to remain on the earth and to finish our job as well.

^ The multitudes of mockers represent the domain of sin and evil. These are the unrighteous people who are living in the kingdom of darkness and who will not remain on the earth. These are the people who continue to live a life of sin and ignorance. They didn't plan to go anywhere in the days of Noah, but they were swept away from the face of the earth. The same will happen with evil people at the end of times.

^ The ark represents the Lord Jesus Christ. It brought protection to God's people when the flood came. Jesus will provide us with complete safety in times of trouble. The ark lifted Noah and his family up from the waves of destruction so that they only observed it from an elevated position. Jesus Christ will lift us up to a higher level of safety and authority in Him in the days of suffering.

^ The flood represents the waters of God's judgment that washed away all evil from the face of the earth. God promised not to flood the earth again with water, but His word will wash away all evil and sin from the face of the earth in the completion of all things.

Matthew 24: 40 Then two men will be in the field: one will be taken and the other left.

KINGDOM AUTHORITY

It is clear that the worker who will keep on working represents the people of God who will remain and finish their job. The worker who was taken away represents evil and unrighteousness, and was removed in judgment. The perfect picture of the story of Noah is one of resilience and staying power.

———————————

There are many Christian books and movies out there that contradict the amazing 'end-time' plan that God has for the church on the earth.

Jesus will never be the 'thief in the night' for His followers. For us, He is the light of our lives. His light is shining through us in a dark world right now. If we vanish, light will be gone and a dark age of demonic governing may loom on the earth.

There are many goodhearted Christians who are actually praying for this day to come. This is never going to happen because Jesus Christ would love us to stay on a little bit longer and to let His light shine in the world. We will remain working in the field. There is no escape from this responsibility. We have to remain on the earth to change this world.

John 17:15 I do not pray that You should take them out of the world, but that You should keep them from the evil one.

Jesus prayed that we would remain strong and very visible in the earth. If the church disappears, so will the glory of God. We are His representatives on the earth. God's glory will fill the whole earth, and this will happen through the glorious church.

Matthew 6:10 Your kingdom come. Your will be done on earth as it is in heaven.

Jesus teaches us to pray for finality and for perfection. We have to long for perfection so that it can be channeled from heaven to the earth. We are on the earth to establish the kingdom of God. We should never attempt to escape our responsibility of managing the earth for God. We are here to establish the beauty and perfection of heaven on planet earth. The only way of escaping this privilege is to die and go to heaven. But we should not plan on taking a short cut. We should plan on traveling on the scenic route with God. There is so much to do, so many places to go, and so many souls to be saved.

The escape mentality is not Biblical. The word 'rapture' does not even occur in the Bible. The 'rapture' theology declares that Jesus Christ will one day return to remove the church from the earth and to transfer all believers to heaven in the twinkling of an eye. This theory contains contradictory concepts of Jesus' teachings. God never intended Noah to vanish, but the evildoers. Jesus will destroy all evil, but righteousness and His righteous people will remain in the earth.

The Bible teaches us that we will meet Jesus one day in a supernatural realm, and that we will be changed in the twinkling of an eye. *(I Corinthians15: 51-54)* But it doesn't say that we will be discharged from the earth. We will be clothed with immortality. We will be reunited with those who died in Christ. We will be perfect; and no one really knows what will happen next!

A vanished church suggests destruction for all people on the earth. We carry the hope of salvation for all the nations. We represent the God who loves all people so much and gave His only Son for them all. We carry the opportunities for reconciliation that people may still receive. We are here on this planet to become the glorious church that will one day enthrone the King of glory. We are here to change the world, penetrate kingdoms of darkness with the light and love of God, and to announce to all the nations that the kingdom of

God is at hand.

We are not going anywhere. Heaven is perfect, but the earth needs perfection. Jesus is not coming back to make things perfect. This is the assignment for the church. We can only complete our assignment if we remain here on earth. How many future generations it may take to complete this task, is unknown. No one knows when finality will take place. Only the Father knows when Jesus Christ will return. Prophets and Apostles don't have a future date for Christ's return, but we have a mandate to work and to keep on working until He returns.

Noah received the opportunity to restore the damage in the earth that Adam caused. It was like a second chance for mankind, and Noah did an excellent job. God wants us to remain on the earth to bring completion and finality to this dimension. Sin and evil were demolished in the flood. It will again be eliminated by the power and glory of heaven, which will be manifested by the sons of God on the earth.

There is nothing to fear and nothing to wait for. Jesus Christ will return to a victorious church. The church needs to step into a global position of realization of this truth. We are here to stay. We are here to take over. We are here to finish our assignment. We will not hide or run away. We refuse to believe the opinions of people. We choose to believe God's word. We will remain on the earth as the remnant of God. We are His chosen, special instruments in the earth. We are not secret agents. We are visible in the kingdom, and we will not go away.

We are here to prepare the way for the King of glory to come back to put His feet again on the dust of the planet that has led to His death. When He returns, all nations will acknowledge who He really is. No one will even think of mocking the King of glory then. He will rule and reign. We will reign with Him. This is the gospel of the kingdom of our Lord Jesus Christ.

11

HEAVEN AND EARTH

Everything is perfect in heaven. This perfection and beauty shines from heaven onto the earth. As God looks down to the earth, He observes a reflection of truth. It is amazing how God can see truth in the mirror of the earth. I am sure that He observes the pain, trouble, and poverty as well, but in His righteousness and from a perfect position, He sees truth. God sowed the truth into the earth when He sent His heavenly Son into our reality.

*Psalms 85: 11 Truth shall spring out of the earth, and righteousness shall look down from heaven.**

* Truth rises from the earth and righteousness smiles down from heaven. (Tay)

When God looks down from heaven today, He observes the mirror image of His only begotten Son. Truth springs up from the earth into the presence of God. It is almost a picture of the earth reaching to heaven, yearning for perfect righteousness. As the Potter molds us into the image of Christ, He just smiles and keeps on smiling. He can see the end from the beginning.

As we connect more with the God of heaven and earth, the perfect picture of heaven will also increasingly be established in the earth dimension. If we live in the righteousness that is shining from heaven, we will reflect the truth to a sinful world.

Psalms 24:1 The earth is the Lord's, and all its fullness, the world and those who dwell therein.

Psalms 115:16 The heaven, even the heavens are the Lord's; But the earth He has given* to the children of men.

* The heaven of heavens is for God, but he put us in charge of the earth.

Gen 1:28 Then God blessed them and God said to them, Be fruitful and multiply; fill the earth and subdue it; have dominion over the fish of the sea, over the birds of the air, and over every living thing that moves on the earth.

We have a heavenly mandate to manage the earth. It is a mandate with no limitations or restrictions. God instructed us to supervise the total spectrum of His earthly creation. We need to remember that the cattle on a thousand hills, the fish in the sea, and all the gold and diamonds in the earth belong to God. Our responsibility is to take care of all His possessions like proper stewards. We need to manage the nature reserves, rivers, mountains and fountains with care. We should look after the animals, forests, and vineyards on the earth. We are supposed to distribute all the natural resources on earth more equally among all its inhabitants, so that all the nations may be blessed. We have not been assigned to manipulate the people on this amazing planet, but to function as the salt of the earth. We are the representatives of the Creator.

We should be visionaries, innovators, and pace-setting leaders who influence the earth (especially the human race), merely by our presence. We are the carriers of His glory and we shine forth His light in all the places of darkness and hopelessness. We show the way, and we point all nations to the Most High God.

———————————-

Genesis 28:12-14 Then he dreamed, and behold a ladder was set up on the earth, and its top reached to heaven; and there the angels of God were ascending and descending on it. And behold, the Lord stood above it and said: In your seed all the families of the earth shall be blessed.

Genesis 28:17 How awesome is this place! This is none other than the house of God, and this is the gate of heaven.

Jacob received this amazing heavenly vision. What a beautiful picture in the Old Testament of the divine connection between heaven and earth. This is a shadow, a pattern, and a forecast of the reality of an open heaven in the lives of God's modern day people. This picture shows the greatness of God, as He stood superiorly above the angels. It shows the kingdom reality of earth linking directly with heaven.

There is such a clear indication in this passage that the blessings of heaven are due to be released to the earth dimension. Angels are activated to convey heavens' best to the people on the earth who need a touch from God. To Jacob this was very real. To him this is how the house of God functions. This is the place where this remarkable ladder connects with earth. Jacob describes this place as the gate of heaven. This gateway has the possibility to open the floodgates of heaven and to release the best of heaven's storehouses into our dry and empty worlds. This is the miracle of God's house; the reality of a supernatural dimension that is closer than we may think.

The gate is open. We have access to this dimension. God is managing all the activities that are taking place. He gives directions and instructions from His heavenly headquarters. Angelic forces are in operation to implement the commands of God from heaven. The people of God need to be activated to touch heaven and to change earth.

The time to be heavenly minded and earthly ineffective is over. To be heavenly minded does not necessarily signify a deep and daily longing to go to heaven. The significance of connecting with heaven is essentially illustrated in the reality of God's people bringing heaven down to earth. It is quite simple. If you have money in the bank, you can go to the ATM at any time, and draw some cash.

We have access to the unlimited resources of heaven's supernatural warehouses. These resources are not to be looked at and to be admired, but it is to be used to our benefit here on earth.

We can dream about heaven and long to actually migrate from earth and all its challenges as soon as possible; or we can connect with the power source of heaven and switch the lights on in a dark society.

———————-

*Matthew 6:10 Your kingdom come, Your will be done on earth# as it is in heaven. ***

* As in heaven, so on earth. (ASV)
# In earth, as it is in heaven. (KJV)

It is clear that Jesus was talking about a connection between two dimensions; heaven and earth. He experienced both dimensions beforehand; He lived in heaven as the Son of

God, and He lived on earth as the Son of man. In this passage, He emphasises the reality that the earth needs what heaven has to offer. The earth desperately needs heaven's perfection and treasures. It needs the perfect peace, power, stability, comfort, and healing that heaven represents. This is why Jesus taught His disciples to pray in this exact manner; 'on earth, as it is in heaven'.

We need to channel all the benefits of heaven down to earth. The river of God flows directly from His throne. This river brings healing to the nations on the earth. *We can transfer heaven's healing and power to the earth dimension through our prayers of faith. If we don't do this, people will just continue to be sick and die.*

Heaven has the solutions to all our existing problems. We can access these supernatural resources today. We don't have to wait any longer. Heaven is ready to give. Heaven is open, and will never close down. The veil between earth and heaven was permanently eliminated by the power of Christ's sacrifice. Access to heaven and all its benefits is granted.

The church can no longer overlook its kingdom responsibility by hoping that Jesus will come back to solve all our problems. To hope and pray that Jesus will take us away on some fantasy road trip to heaven would be totally against God's plan of releasing heavens' best to earth. By wishing that we would go to heaven before we have changed earth for the better, we are merely fantasizing; and we display zero accountability in terms of our earthly mandate. With such ignorance in our thinking, God's instruction for us to change earth will be completely violated.

Matthew 16:19 And I will give you the keys of the kingdom of heaven, and whatever you bind on earth will be bound in heaven, and whatever you loose on earth will be loosed in heaven.*

* The Realm of heaven, and whatever you prohibit on earth

will be prohibited in heaven, and whatever you permit on earth will be permitted in heaven. (Mof)

* And whatever you forbid on earth will be held in Heaven to be forbidden, and whatever you allow on earth will be held in Heaven to be allowed. (TCNT)

* And whatever you bind on earth shall remain bound in heaven, and whatever you loose on earth shall remain loosed in heaven. (Wey)

* And whatever you bind [declare to be improper and unlawful] on earth must be what is already bound in heaven; and whatever you loose [declare lawful] on earth must be what is already loosed in heaven. (Amp)

Adam received the keys to paradise- God's domain of perfection and beauty. Sadly Adam handed this gift to Satan through disobeying God's command, and by succumbing to sin. Mankind was then cast out of this perfect relationship with God, and the cunning snake snatched the keys from Adam and Eve. Darkness prevailed for many ages to come.

Sin reigned in the lives of many people for millenniums. Wicked kings established their evil kingdoms on earth, until Jesus came to the rescue. God's plan of salvation brought healing to the nations on the earth.

When Jesus gave his life and was buried for three days, He descended into Hades and confiscated the keys of paradise from the possession of the prince of evil. He later presented these keys to Peter and the church. By receiving the keys from the Lord Jesus Christ on this day, Peter accepted the responsibility to manage the keys, and to utilise it effectively.

Today, this extraordinary privilege is ours. Yes, the keys of the kingdom are currently under the ownership of the church of the Lord Jesus Christ. We have the authority to unlock blessings and heavenly forces that can shape the destiny of many countries as well as billions of people on our planet. We can eliminate the forces of sin and shame that repeatedly attempt to torture and intimidate the church.

By using the keys effectively, heaven's doors will be opened and the fullness of heaven will invade earth. Heaven's greatness is accessible but the doors of all the abundance need to be opened by God's kingdom people through faith and prayer. We should step into the supernatural arena of heaven's glory. It is time to unlock the doors of health, success, riches, opportunities, blessings and wisdom in heaven, and receive these amazing kingdom benefits right here and now on planet earth.

Imagine how we may take time out of the equation. Imagine how we can make proper financial decisions. Imagine how our children can follow the exact pathway of God for their future.

Imagine the glory of God coming down from heaven. We sang the songs and we preached the sermons. Let's put our money where our mouths are, and get the job done by the grace of God- in the name of Jesus Christ, our Lord and King.

Although the Pentecostal revivalists and evangelists made many mistakes through the decades, it will be of no spiritual advantage for future generations if we major on these mistakes. One thing they proclaimed accurately and with no disgrace is summarized by the words of a very old chorus:

"It's coming down, down, down- it's coming down.

The glory of the Lord is coming down. When the saints

begin to pray, the Lord shall have His way.

The glory of the Lord is coming down."

I don't think we should settle for less. It would break the heart of the Father if we reject His flow of goodness and blessings into our lives. All our twenty first century reasoning and intellectual prejudices can easily limit the incredible promises that heaven holds. When God's river will start flowing from the throne room in heaven, there will be no force that would be able to stop this incredible flood.

Church leaders may prefer to make no or limited reference to this heavenly outpouring, but the people in the kingdom of God will proclaim, display, and confirm the reality of heaven on planet earth. If we miss out because of our lack of faith, the generations to follow will reap the benefits of heaven's perfection.

—————————————-

Isaiah 66:1 Heaven is my throne, and earth is my footstool.*

* The Lord says, Heaven is the seat of my power, and earth is the resting-place for my feet. (Bas)

God has done an amazing job with creation. He designed the whole universe in six days, and then decided to have a good rest on the seventh day. God was completely satisfied with His work, and took a position of rest until this very day. Amazingly, He chose the earth as His footstool. This displays His approval of designing planet earth, and more specifically regenerating mankind according to His own image. God's position of rest, demonstrates His complete reign and sovereign rule over everything. God is not nervous and cannot be intimidated. He has not been voted into any position, and will never be voted out. He is seated on His throne, and will forever display His might and authority to all of creation.

Revelation 21:1 Now I saw a new heaven and a new earth, for the first heaven and the first earth had passed away.

Isaiah 65:17 For behold, I create new heavens and a new earth; and the former shall not be remembered or come to mind.

Nothing turns old when God is around. I sometimes wonder why God would plan on renewing heaven, as it is a perfect place with no pain, sin or shame. Maybe God is just into restoration. Maybe He just likes to keep on creating new things.

On the other hand, it would be much easier to comprehend the idea of God restoring the earth. Earth is a planet with dust and deserts, fire and fury, sin and shame, deceit and destruction. It is the place where Satan disembarked after being suspended from heaven.

Earth is a place of intriguing contrasts:

* It is a place of demonic rebellion but it is also the place where Jesus Christ was resurrected.
* It is place with land and seas, night and day, winter and summer, mountains and valleys.
* It is a place with wicked and righteous people, selfish and humble leaders, violent dictators and peacemaking governors.
* It is a place where some people chase after lustful cravings in the dark while others are praying for a global revival.

In the midst of these contrasts and seeming confusions, God keeps on working behind the scenes. His work involves renewing the earth. His plan is to restore all things to its original form of perfection. God has no intention of handing the earth over to any antichrist, world-ruler, dictator, or even the devil himself. In fact, God already designated His followers to take responsibility for the supervision of His magnificent earth.

Isaiah 66:22 For as the new heavens and the new earth which I make shall remain before Me, says the Lord, so shall your descendants and your name remain.

Psalms 37:9 For evil men will be cut off, but those who hope in the Lord will inherit the land. (NIV)

KINGDOM AUTHORITY

Psalms 37:11 But the meek will inherit the land and enjoy great peace. (NIV)

Psalms 37: 22 Those the Lord blesses will inherit the land, but those he curses will be cut off. (NIV)

Psalms 37: 29 The righteous will inherit the land and dwell in it forever. (NIV)

In these verses we found such a wonderful assurance. God is not about to destroy the beauty of His own creation. In fact, He creates new things and He restores old things. Just as He will create new heavens and a new earth, God will bless His people generationally. There is no way we will be destroyed. We will remain on the earth. We should thankfully accept our inheritance. What a blessing to be heirs of the Father and co-heirs with Jesus Christ. Jesus died on the cross, and we are the beneficiaries of God's heavenly blessings; now and forever.

It is too good to be true, but it is the truth. We are the recipients of God's eternal mercy and grace. God will renew the earth, and He will renew us. Our descendants will never be blotted out. We were made in God's image and His image will remain eternally. We belong to Him and will continually be part of His remnant. We are the ones who will always remain. Evil will vanish, sin will be destroyed, but we will remain in the land forever.

As discussed in a previous chapter, we now understand that nobody really knows how things will play out when Christ returns. I don't think it is necessary for us to study all the interpretations of the new era. Our longing should not be 'heaven' as an insurance for our eternal destiny. Our concern should be the millions of people on this amazing planet who are still living without purpose and salvation.

I am so thankful that we are not living in the Old Testament times, or in the dark ages, or even when the Apostles were wandering here on earth. Today is the best time to be alive. Today is the day of salvation to all the nations of the earth. I can hear a multitude of saints in the heavenly dimension proclaim: "Amen and amen!"

12

THE REVEALED SONS OF GOD

I have been a football enthusiast for as long as I can remember. I am still a dedicated follower of the South African Springbok rugby team, a team that had to endure the challenge of being excluded from international sport for a very long time. I have childhood memories of the rivalry between the Springboks and the mighty New Zealand All Blacks. As a ten year old, I used to study newspaper and magazine articles about the players' abilities and training programs. I gained knowledge of their height, weight, and match statistics. Amazingly, the Springboks survived all those years of exclusion and political drama and became the world champions with their first appearance in a rugby World Cup in 1995.

In Australia, I was introduced to many football codes that I had never known about as a child. Many football heroes describe how they had always dreamt of playing for their state or national teams. There are huge challenges for any team in any sport in terms of becoming the best. A team has to have the desire to become a champion team against all odds. Statistics, physical size of opponents, media information, play conditions (such as altitude and inclement weather), and preparation time should have zero effect on a champion team. It should all be about belief, pride, and attitude.

In the modern game of football, every team wants to play in the grand final. The grand final is the climax of the season's competition and teams that compete in regular tournaments are not as well known until they perform well in a particular season. Teams only make a name for themselves when they advance to the finals or play-offs, but especially if they go right through to the grand final. Winning the grand final will place any team in the hall of champions.

It is impossible to reach this ultimate stage in any championship if your mindset is not focused towards victory. You have to talk, walk, eat, work, play, and live for this glorious moment. Sport teams with a winning mentality, a high work ethic, and an effective coaching and management staff, are formidable competitors.

Romans 8:19 For the earnest expectation* of the creation eagerly waits for the revealing of the sons of God.

* For the longing of the creation looks eagerly for the time when [the glory of] the sons of God shall be revealed. (Con)
* The whole creation is on tiptoe to see the wonderful sight of the sons of God coming into their own. (Phi)
* For [even the whole] creation [all nature] waits expectantly and longs earnestly for God's sons to be made known [waits for the revealing, the disclosing of their sonship]. (Amp)

The church did not just enter a competition hoping for the best. We entered the competition of life knowing that we will be the champions. There is nothing that can change this outcome- even if we don't believe it, or feel it, or dream it- it is going to happen. *The victory was accomplished over two thousand years ago and the outcome has already been determined. The church will be handed the trophy. We will celebrate the victory.*

Knowing this doesn't imply that the church should sit back and hope for the best. This victory has to be enforced by faith. We have to proclaim the victory in our daily lives, living like champions. We should show the world that there is hope in the midst of trouble, and that there is a light at the end of the tunnel; indeed, a light in the tunnel! Jesus Christ has finished His work, and we have the privilege of being His ambassadors of grace, love and victory.

We are not just trying to survive in all the turmoil, pain, and challenges that life throws at us. We are more than conquerors in all situations. We basically play every game knowing there will be a positive outcome. Jesus never said it would be easy, but He gave us the textbook with all the rules, ideas, practical hints and strategies for the game.

Thinking about failure, having fear of the next step, and hoping for possible escape will lead to unnecessary struggles, pain and misery in our spiritual walk, and we may miss out on living life as overcomers. There are no short cuts to the grand final. It includes many tough battles that will leave us with scars and wounds. Playing to reach the ultimate grand final as a Christian requires faith, love, a kingdom mindset as well as a lifestyle of walking with God.

This season will be the ultimate display of victory- the time when we will be revealed us the sons of God; the day when the sons will reveal the Son. And every tongue will confess the Lordship of Jesus Christ as well as the true reign of His kingdom on the earth.

God's plan is for His sons to be revealed to all creation as the ultimate team of champions. Jesus' plan is for His body (the church) to grow into a position of maturity and perfection. We compete against all forces of darkness. The ultimate price is eternal glory. The stakes are much higher than in any sport. We are focused on eternal rewards and the celebration of our amazing victory in Christ Jesus our Lord.

God the Father is our 'team manager', Jesus Christ is our 'head coach', and the Holy Spirit is our 'team psychologist'. The chosen team consists of all the sons of God. All the newspapers, television networks, social networking systems and even the 'doom prophets' from all walks of life, will announce that the victory belongs to the sons of God. Before the season has started, right through to the grand final and beyond, there can only be one champion team- the sons of God!

———————————

*Romans 8:22 For we know that the whole creation groans and labors with birth pangs together until now. ***

* We are now manifesting what Jesus Christ already has accomplished.
* We are now revealing the reality of Christ's reconciliation deed.
* We are now establishing His finished work.
* We are now the mobile miracles of the Man of mercy.
* We are now the hands and feet of the King whose hands and feet were pierced.
* This is the season wherein we will give birth to the greatest spiritual revival the world has ever seen.

The manifestation of the sons of God is likened to a spiritual birth that will bring joy and peace into the earth. This Scripture offers a clear picture of expectancy such as the longing of a pregnant woman waiting to give birth to a new life. She carries the hope and anticipation of the birth of a child for nine months beforehand. This season of waiting feels to her like an eternity, but she knows the wait is worthwhile and that months of preparation, dreaming and even the physical discomfort and tension will turn into a joyous reality. When she holds her baby in her arms, the mother experiences all the joy and peace that only heaven can deliver.

It is impossible for me to describe the labor pains my wife endured while she gave birth to our children, but I remember the unbelievable moments of glory when our child was finally born. We were both filled with joy and peace—our child was revealed to this world, and the waiting was over. An indescribable cloud of satisfaction and thankfulness surrounded us.

Creation itself has a deep and hidden longing for something significant, supernatural and wonderful to happen.

Creation anticipates the moment when the real sons of God will appear. His human warriors will be made manifest as the true disciples of the living God, as they take their place and responsibility in His army. The earth yearns for this day of renewal and restoration.

In this day and age, people want to see reality, not fake and false doctrines or religious obligations. The world is looking for people who represent and demonstrate real love and grace. The longing for perfection is written into the heart of every person and creation itself. Everybody would love to see a little bit of paradise again.

People don't just want to listen to sermons; they want to see some action. They want answers to their prayer requests, healing for their hurting hearts and comfort for their emotional turmoil. People need relationship with the revealed sons of God so that they can be introduced to the Son of God.

We are not called to be secret agents in this world, but manifested sons of the living God. We are called to demonstrate the grace, goodness, and glory of God in the earth. This is our privilege. When we succeed in this, many people will turn

141

to God, and many more sons of God will be birthed into His kingdom.

To be manifested or revealed to creation as the sons of God is not for our own glory. It will not happen because we are so wonderful or anointed. It will happen as part of God's restoration plan for the earth. We are called to introduce and implement revival in the earth as God initiated it at the time of Christ's resurrection.

We need to perform miracles, heal people, forgive sins, and bring healing to the nations on His behalf. The sons of God need to arise from their passive ways and their religious activities. We need to be revealed as the true ambassadors of Christ Jesus in the earth. We need to accurately represent the amazing works of Christ in our churches, communities and work places.

We should have an expectation for this to happen. Creation is longing for this global restoration. The church should be praying for this revival. The church should be preparing for the sons of God to be revealed. The church should be preaching the gospel of the kingdom to all the earth so that Jesus Christ will return in His glory and splendor.

2 Thessalonians 1:10 speaks about Christ being glorified in His saints.

We should complete what we have been called to do.

————————————-

Revelation 16:17 Then the seventh angel poured out his bowl into the air; and a loud voice came out of the temple of heaven, from the throne, saying, 'It is done!'

Jesus Christ accomplished the ultimate victory on the cross for all mankind by laying down His own life, dying the most horrifying death. He did everything to bring salvation and reconciliation to mankind. He died for the sin and shame of all people through all ages. His last words on that rugged cross were: 'It is finished!' *(John 19:30)* And it is.

These words still echo through the corridors of time, bringing assurance of salvation as well as the promise of spiritual completion to the sons of God. All our pain, battles, and turmoil will be transformed into ecstatic joy. *Every day with Jesus will bring us closer to perfect maturity in His amazing kingdom.* There is nothing we need to perform or accomplish on our own.

No brilliant act, intellectual discovery, charismatic speech, sacrificial effort of grace or mercy— absolutely nothing— can alter the indescribable perfection of His selfless act. All we need to do is believe what Jesus has said and done. We have to believe that Jesus Christ has accomplished everything. Now we need to put our faith into action and live our lives from a 'finished work' perspective. We shouldn't be observed like unfit players in the start of the season, but like well-prepared champions who already have one hand on the trophy.

Ecclesiastes 3:11a He has made everything beautiful in its time. Also He has put eternity in their hearts.

God declares the end from the beginning, and from ancient times things that are not yet done. *(Isaiah 46:10)* He does not operate in chronological time, but lives outside of time. Jesus Christ is the Beginning and the End, the One who is and was and is to come. *(Rev 1:8)* His works were finished from the foundation of the world. (*Hebrews 4:3*)

———————————-

Acts 3:19-21 Repent therefore and be converted, that your sins may be blotted out, so that times of refreshing may come in the presence of the Lord, and that He may send Jesus Christ, who was preached to you before, whom heaven must receive until *the times of restoration of all things,* which God has spoken by the mouth of all His holy prophets since the world began.*

Jesus was sent to the world to bring about the forgiveness of sin for mankind. He completed this assignment as the Son of God in human form. Jesus died and rose again. He ascended into heaven where He sits on His throne at the right hand of the throne of God. There is nothing more Jesus can do to add to our right standing before God because He has already paid the full price and completed His assignment in full.

Jesus will not return to 'fix things' for us— fixing the world was the task He set us when He told us to make disciples of all nations *(Matthew 28:19)*. He will return to a glorious church that will accept her responsibility to reconcile and restore all things in the earth.

* The 'all things' can include:

- The nations in the earth.
- Political arenas and business sectors.
- Governmental and educational institutions.
- Family life and friendships.
- Sport, art, culture and music.
- Every church, missionary organization and Bible study group.
- All the 'kids programs' all over the world.
- All groups of people from diverse cultures, tribes, languages and religion.
- All plant and animal life.

All things will be restored to their original state of perfection. Paradise was perfect. God's original plan was perfect. Adam and Eve were perfect. Adam walked and talked with God as he did with Eve. Adam walked and talked with lions and bears. They had no worries. Everything was perfect.

This perfection was spoiled when arrogance, rebellion and sin came on the scene. Adam blamed Eve, who blamed the snake. Perfection changed into pathetic shame. The harmony of their relationship with God and each other was transformed into loneliness and pain. Adam and Eve were exiled from the garden. Their connection with God was lost and they found themselves in need of a Savior. The once perfect situation needed restoration that only the Son of God could ever bring. Thankfully, God already had a plan for the second Adam (His Son Jesus Christ) to appear and to reconcile people into a perfect relationship with Him.

Jesus Christ became this mediator between fallen man and perfect God. He came to restore all brokenness and pain. He came to reunite mankind with their Creator. Jesus Christ became the sinless Adam. He initiated the possibility of an amazing restoration on the earth while at the same time completing all the work that was necessary to make it possible.

Jesus has commissioned us with making it happen and we received the wonderful Holy Spirit, who operates in all locations, in all people, at any given time. We also have constant angelic assistance, a loving Father who shepherds us daily with love and care, and heavenly authority to pursue the kingdom of God and to get the job done.

Elijah lived a life of miracles and then passed the baton to Elisha. Elijah left in glory and his mantle fell down to the earth. Elisha picked up this mantle and walked in a glorious anointing, doing twice as many miracles compared with his predecessor. *(Second chapter of the second book of Kings)*

Jesus lived a miraculous life, proclaiming a kingdom that will never be destroyed. Amazingly He passed the baton to you and me. He wants us to walk in His glory. *God wants us to establish the finished work of Christ on earth. He wants us to establish the kingdom with more miracles, healings and salvations that could ever be recorded on this planet, so that all men will see His glory.*

KINGDOM AUTHORITY

We are elected by divine authority to bring finality to this dimension. We are chosen by God to implement the kingdom purposes He has for the earth. We are co-workers and representatives of Jesus Christ himself. We have received the Holy Spirit power that will enable us to complete this heavenly assignment on the earth.

This is our cause. This is why we are alive on planet earth. This is our grand final, and we are on the winning team. If we will embrace our part in preparing, thinking and behaving like champions, we can live the adventure as the revealed sons of the living God.

13

THE REVELATION OF JESUS CHRIST

This is the name of the last book in the Bible. God certainly knows how to keep the best for last. This wonderful last book of the Bible is actually about the revealing of the Lord Jesus Christ. Inaccurate and immature teachings about this book regularly emphasize the passages about dragons, devils, and destruction. Through some bizarre teachings, many church people and leaders have sadly been misinformed about this amazing book.

Instead of acknowledging and balancing past, present, and futuristic information, scholars decided to interpret the whole book as *only futuristic*. They analyze the information with clever reasoning and pre-conceived ideas. They explain events using chronological time frames as well as futuristic predictions. Nowadays, many church people categorically believe in apocalyptic events as described in books and movies. The Hollywood interpretation of the book of

Revelation is regularly more acceptable in the life of the church, than the godly truth.

The only method we have to counterfeit the false doctrine about this book is to receive a revelation from Christ about the Christ of the book of Revelation. With supernatural Holy Spirit clarification, most pre-conceived ideas people may have would be turned the right side up.

Sound doctrine is one of the pillars in the kingdom of God. We can no longer believe in 'Old wives' tales, and think we will penetrate the kingdom of darkness. Inaccurate doctrinal believe-systems will lead to ineffective Christian living. However, having no doctrinal views at all represent ignorance and foolishness. Ignorance in the kingdom is not a valid excuse for immaturity, false teachings and basic lethargy. Foolishness is nothing else than deliberate refusal to grow up in the kingdom dimension.

People say things like:

- *'Nobody genuinely knows much about the final stages for the church.'*
- *' I have read this opinion in a book.'*
- *'It doesn't really matter.'*
- *'Revelation is the most difficult book in the Bible.'*
- *Revelation is just about dragons and beasts and it is almost too scary to read.'*
- *'I heard some confusing sermons about Revelation and I am therefore not interested to read it.'*
- *'God doesn't really want us to understand these things.'*

Having a revelation about book of Revelation brings kingdom simplicity into practice. This simple understanding about God's finality and His perfect plan to bring closure to this dimension will bring peace and freedom to the mind of the believer. This revelation about Jesus Christ is more than a book. It is a faith manifestation about the goodness of God, and not a concerning and stressful anticipation of the end of the world.

Traditional man-made ideas about this last Bible book need to be weighed against the truth of the kingdom. 'Good' just sounds better than 'bad'. And there is no way around this statement: 'Jesus is greater than the devil.'

Putting all pre-conceived ideas aside, and without digging too deep into head knowledge, let's look at the basic essence of the chapters of the book called 'The Revelation of Jesus Christ':

> *Chapter one* describes the Son of Man in the beauty of His splendor. He is the First and the Last and He lives forevermore.

> *Chapter two and three* illustrates the spiritual condition of the seven churches represented on the earth. The angel of the Lord gives warnings, encouragements, and hope to the churches on planet earth. This clearly shows the reality of the church overcoming all obstacles, and having the potential of actually ruling the earth as God's chosen representatives.

> *Chapter four* displays the perfect heaven, and the One who sits on the throne.

> Every creature in *chapter five* worships Him who sits on the throne; as well as the Lamb. The redeemed of the Lord are mentioned here as kings and priests who will reign on the earth.

> *Chapter six* reveals the authority of the Lamb of God as He opens the six seals of the judgment and supremacy of God. Judgment includes freedom, peace, and the conquering of many battles.

> *Chapter seven* displays the sealing of the servants of God on their foreheads. Here God demonstrates His governmental authority- structure by referring to the

twelve tribes of Israel. Each tribe represents thousands of people in multiple generations. Also, we need to understand that 'twelve' is the number of God's perfect governance in the kingdom dimension. God still governs the earth using this number. We operate with a twelve-hour day, twelve-hour night, and twelve-month calender system. Chapter seven also illustrates a great multitude of people and angels worshipping God before the throne.

Chapter eight describes the opening of the seventh seal. The wonder of prayer is described in detail, revealing the reality of the prayers of the saints being offered to God. It is great to see this heavenly vision of how our prayers are actually received in heaven; and having amazing results on earth.

Those who did not receive the seal of God on their foreheads are in for a bit of trouble under the reign of the governor of the bottomless pit. *Chapter nine* describes the torment and shame awaiting the people who are not fully committed to God.

In *chapter ten* another mighty angel displays the powerful connection between heaven and earth. He connected heaven and earth with a beautiful rainbow, glorious clouds, radiant sunbeams, as well as pillars of fire. In the midst of this splendor, the angel announced that the mystery of God would be fulfilled. This mystery is now revealed; and this is the amazing mystery of Christ!

In *chapter eleven* the seventh angel declares that the kingdom of our Lord and of His Christ will overtake all worldly kingdoms, and that Christ will reign forever and ever.

Chapter twelve announces that the kingdom of our God, and the power of His Christ have come. The supremacy of Christ is declared after a heavenly war wherein Michael and his angels conquered Satan and his angels. The emphasis is not warfare, but the reality of God's people living as overcomers. This victory was accomplished by the fact that Jesus was crucified as a Lamb who gave His life to save the world.

Chapter thirteen highlights the patience and the faith of the saints whose names are written in the Book of Life of the Lamb who was slayed. The mark and the number of the beast mentioned in this chapter, have no eternal effect on the saints. The saints are not marked by a man, but by the living God. We are marked with God's perfect number (seven), which implies maturity and perfection. The number of man (six), represents the sum of all possible humanistic ideologies and worldly influences. God's people are sealed and secured, as they are born into the kingdom of God. It is impossible for us to be 'remarked' by this number of the 'beast'!

Chapter fourteen presents the Lamb standing on Mount Zion. A new song is sung as thundering heavenly worship is recorded here. This chapter describes the everlasting gospel being presented to every nation, tribe, tongue, and peoples on the earth. It also pictures Jesus Christ in glorious splendor with a golden crown on His head. It also describes harvest time on the earth with nations turning to Jesus Christ. Most importantly, it describes the trampling of the winepress outside the city, and the blood that came out of the winepress. Jesus Christ was crucified outside the city, and His blood was shed for all the people on the earth.

We read in *chapter fifteen* how the temple was filled

with the glory and the power of God. Here, heaven was opened and the eternal connection with earth was established. The Lord God Almighty, and the King of the saints are worshipped and glorified. This chapter confirms that all nations shall come and worship before the King.

Chapter sixteen describes the greatest war ever. During this war, all the sin and shame of mankind, all the evil and hell-fire from Satan, and all the wrath of God were poured out on one place, Armageddon. Jesus Christ faced the fiercest of all battles, having been punished for all the shame, sin, sickness, and evil that could ever exist on the face of the earth. Amazingly, there was a great earthquake, thundering and lightning, and a loud voice came out of the temple of heaven, saying, 'It is done!' When Jesus Christ proclaimed these words, He announced His finished work. The war has ended. It is finished.

Chapter seventeen reveals Jesus Christ as the Lord of lords and the King of kings. It also reveals His chosen and faithful followers who are forever with Him.

Another angel announces the fall of Babylon in *chapter eighteen.* This angel comes down from heaven with great authority, and illuminates the earth with his glory. All worldly systems will come to a fall, but the glory of God will fill the whole earth as the waters cover the sea.

The King of kings and the Lord of lords is once again the center of attention in *chapter nineteen.* Here, heaven is opened and Jesus Christ appears in majestic array. His eyes were like fire flames, and He wears many crowns.He is clothed with a robe dipped in blood, and His name is called 'The Word of God'. The marriage feast of the Lamb is announced and the 'beast' of our human, sinful nature is captivated and destroyed.

Chapter twenty visualizes the torment that the devil and his army of demons will have to endure forever and ever. But, as in every other chapter, the focus is mainly on Him who sits on the great white throne, as well as on Christ and His representatives who will reign with Him.

Chapter twenty-one displays the descending of the city of heaven to the earth dimension, and God making His abode with mankind. The governmental rule of this city will release the glory of the Lord into the earth. This city is illuminated by the glory of God, and Christ, the Lamb, is its light. The unity between God and man in the new earth is emphasized by the description of the unity between Jesus Christ and the Church. There will be many nations on the new earth, and they shall walk in the light of the city of God. The city of God is not limited to time and space, but is an eternal dwelling for all who believes in the name of the Lord Jesus Christ.

Chapter twenty-two describes the ultimate perfection that all believers hope for. We will see Jesus Christ face to face, and there will be no more curses, pain, or shame. Living water will flow constantly from the throne of God and the Lamb. There shall be no night in the eternal, perfect kingdom, and we shall reign forever and ever. This chapter gives us just a foretaste of what perfection looks like, as the time to strive for perfection is at hand.

The last Book in the Bible reveals Jesus Christ, the King of Glory, to the nations of the earth. Every chapter proclaims His majesty and splendor in heaven and on earth. We do not have to afraid of the devil in the children's Bible where he is illustrated as the reddish creature with horns and a tail, and a fork in his hand.

The Book of Revelation describes the devil as a conquered foe, and a defeated enemy. There is no place in the kingdom of God for the honoring of the fallen one. It is a waste of time and energy to discuss the life story of the enemy of our souls. All we need to understand about the devil is that he has been deported from heaven because of his arrogance and rebellion against God. He functioned on the earth as a poisonous snake, and brought evil, sin, and shame to mankind through the ages. His evil nature and relentless deceit and craftiness saw him surviving many generations, and sending many people to eternal separation from God.

The sinful choices of mankind through thousands of years transformed the snake into an intimidating dragon. Misinterpretations of the book of The Revelation of Jesus Christ by church leaders influenced many people to believe that the devil is well and alive on planet earth. People couldn't stop writing books about dragons, demons, devils, evil beasts and destruction. The church wasted enough time through the centuries by embracing the doctrines of demons. The devil and his demon army deserve no attention from the church.

We should never forget that Jesus Christ has intervened our earthly dimension with all His might. When He died on Calvary, He crushed the head of the devil. Shedding His blood for the sins of all mankind, Jesus Christ gave archangel Michael the permission to make Armageddon a reality. Dragons, beasts, and demons were destroyed in a three-day war that would make 'World War I & 2' combined look like a recess at   Kindergarten. This wonderful book describes the beauty of the unity between God and man.

When Jesus Christ will return to the earth in glory, the glorious church on earth will welcome the King of heaven. The saints through the ages will return with Him to unite with their earthly bodies. God will make His abode with mankind, and we will reign on the earth. This is what kingdom people believe. We will rule, celebrate, and judge the nations.

The good news for people, who are not too excited about singing for eternity, is that there will be so much more to do. Instead of looking at our clean mansions the whole day, we will judge angels, enjoy new heavens, and explore the long awaiting beauty of the rest of God's creation. We will have no more dramas, no more tears, and no more sickness. Death will have no more effect, and we will be perfected. After this amazing reunion between God and His people, we will receive fresh instructions to pursue eternity with God.

14

CONCLUSION

God created everything for a specific purpose and His ultimate design for mankind is for the nations to give Him glory and honor. We can establish God's purpose for the earth through the activation of our faith in our daily lives. We have to obey God's instructions wholeheartedly. We have to seek the kingdom of God first. God and His amazing kingdom have to be our number one priority in this life.

*Genesis 1:28 Then God blessed them, and God said to them, 'Be fruitful and multiply: fill the earth and subdue it; have dominion over the fish of the sea, over the birds of the air, and over every living thing that moves on the earth.' ***

*** And God blessed them saying: 'Increase and multiply and fill the earth and subdue it.' [Sept]

In the very first book of the Bible, God commanded us to have dominion over His creation.

We were created in His image and this means that we are people who can design, create, initiate, lead, govern and judge. The church is a 'sleeping giant' who needs to wake up and display the glory of God to all nations. Although our initial state of perfection in the Garden of Eden was ruined by sin and shame, we currently have the opportunity to restore creation to its original condition of glory.

Isaiah 40:2a Speak comfort to Jerusalem, and cry out to her, that her warfare is ended.

*Isaiah 40:5a The glory of the Lord shall be revealed, and all flesh shall see it together. ***

* The glory of the Lord will be seen by all mankind together. [Tay]

This passage from the very centre of the Bible also reveals the fact that God has indeed paved the way for His people on the earth today.

We can subsequently walk on this path of reconciliation concerning what God initially intended for us. We don't have to fight anymore. The battle belongs to the Lord and we can now demonstrate victorious lifestyles to all people around us. The glory of God will finally be displayed through His human representatives on the earth.

Heaven connected with earth when Moses 'the Law representative', Elijah 'the Prophetic voice', and Jesus, the Son of the living God simultaneously appeared on a high mountain. Jesus was transfigured before the eyes of Peter, James, and John. Jesus' face shone like the sun and His clothes became as white as light. This was a glimpse of heaven and the voice of the Father declared: 'This is my beloved Son, in whom I am well pleased. Hear Him!' *(Matthew 17:5b)* Then Jesus touched them and they could *only see Him.* Moses and Elijah faded. Although they were wonderful servants of God, the perfection of heaven is encapsulated in one person only, Jesus Christ.

Revelation 22:4,5 They shall see His face, and His name shall be on their foreheads. There shall be no night there... And they shall reign forever and ever.

The perfection of heaven is beautifully illustrated in the very last chapter of the Bible.

We are currently seated in heavenly places with Jesus Christ our Lord. *(Ephesians 2:6)* We are connected to the throne room of heaven, the wellspring of life, as well as the tree of life; to produce fruit on the earth that will bring healing to the nations.

Our assignment is not to long for heaven, but to bring salvation and healing to the people on this planet. This can only be accomplished if we focus our full attention on Jesus Christ. He is both the author, and the finisher of our faith. He is the water of life. He is the light of this world. He is the way, the truth, and the life. He does not want us to dream about golden streets and dust-free mansions. He wants us to preach the reality of the kingdom gospel to all nations. It is actually all about Jesus!

——————————————

Whilst many Christians are still conscientiously and religiously doing what they have been used to for so many years, something incredible is happening behind the scenes. God is doing a new thing in the earth. This is something that only those who enter the kingdom reality will be able to grasp and embrace. Nicodemus was a Bible scholar but Jesus told him to be born again if he wanted to see and enter the kingdom dimension. *(John 3:1-6)*

Instead of dreaming and singing about heaven, we should proclaim salvation in the dark streets of our cities.

Conversely, instead of holding on to 'doom and gloom' philosophies and inaccurate doctrinal opinions, we should be preaching the word of God in season and out of season. We are not perfect, but we are on our way to perfection.

The barriers of denominationalism, religiosity, doctrinal ignorance, false humility and pride are falling. There is currently a warrior cry in all the churches, cities, and nations on this planet. This is a cry of desperation, hunger, and worship. This is an expression of a desire that people have for the kingdom of God to take charge in all societies today.

We are called to bring the kingdom of God into the earthly realm. We may be the generation who will transform the nations into the image and glory of the living God. We are alive on planet earth to establish this amazing kingdom, and to infiltrate this world with the love, peace, healing, and glory of our God!

Petrus and His Wife Millanie (Above)

ABOUT THE AUTHOR

Petrus is pursuing God. He never planned immigrating or even writing a book. Petrus believes that this is a new season and that reading his book 'Kingdom Authority' will release people into the plans and purposes that God has for their lives. Petrus declares that God is doing this right now on planet earth. God is calling kingdom warriors to be revealed as His sons in the earth. No more intimidations by the doctrines of demons. This is the moment heaven is waiting for. We were born into the kingdom for a time such as this. We possess the keys to unlock the floodgates of heaven into this earthly dimension.

In quite a conservative suburb,Throne Life Ministries was started with only a few people. His vision of bringing people of all cultures together was accomplished within this period. People from many different languages, diverse cultural backgrounds, and even different countries assembled to express the ever increasing kingdom of God. With his migration to Australia, in 2008, the church has been handed over to Judah Ministries International. Petrus is currently a teacher at Sunrise Christian College in Adelaide, Australia.

Petrus is a Bible teacher and is passionate about the kingdom of God. He loves the Word and teaches sound kingdom doctrine. Petrus planted and pastored churches in South Africa, and are now living the kingdom reality in Adelaide, South Australia.

Timeline of Credits:
Petrus started of being the Senior Pastor in
Riversdale AFM. (1994-1996)
Petrus, then became an Associate Pastor in the much larger church in
Beyerspark, Johannesburg. (1996-1997)
And, he was asked to be the Senior Pastor of the
Queensburgh AFM congregation. (1997-2002)
Petrus was the founder of Throne Life Ministries, a Multicultural church in the diverse city of Durban in KwaZulu Natal, South Africa. (2003-2007)